Grace BROKE THE CHAINS

Dear Estelle,
May God bless you as you read this. You are special —
Susan

SUSAN ELIZABETH BUTCHER

Grace Broke the Chains

Trilogy Christian Publishers A Wholly Owned Subsidiary of Trinity Broadcasting Network

2442 Michelle Drive Tustin, CA 92780

Cover design by: Trilogy

For information about special discounts for bulk purchases, please contact Trilogy Christian Publishing.

Manufactured in the United States of America

10 9 8 7 6 5 4 3 2 1

Library of Congress Cataloging-in-Publication Data is available.

ISBN: 978-1-68556-372-1

E-ISBN: 978-1-68556-373-8

Dedication

To my Lord and Savior, Jesus Christ, who brought me up from the miry clay and set my feet on the solid rock. Thank You for saving me and allowing me to share my personal relationship with You with anyone and everyone. I am truly humbled by what You have done for me and continue to do. Praise You, Jesus!

And

To all those who have encouraged me in my walk with Jesus Christ and my commitment to serve Him through the gifts and talents He has given me. Thank you from the bottom of my heart. You have truly made a difference in my life. This book would not have come to fruition without you.

Acknowledgments

I have so many people to thank; I don't know where to start. I will begin by thanking my Lord and Savior, Jesus Christ, who has bestowed on me the gift of writing, along with the ability to share my faith. I thank Him for the overwhelming opportunities He has given me and for the gift of storytelling. My only hope is that I have not failed to do what He has called me to. This book is truly His and only because of Him. He has walked with me from the beginning to the end.

Along with this, my deepest gratitude goes to those who have walked beside me—from the People Encouraging People team at my church, who labored with me by reading each and every devotion and giving me counsel, to my pastors, who stood by me watching how Jesus worked, to Ceil, Andrew, Jess, and many friends who have encouraged me along the way. Most of all, to those who invested in this book, showing me the love, concern, and faithfulness of themselves and their willingness to be of use to Jesus. I am indebted to all of you. This book is for Him and for you. To write this book would have been beyond impossible without you!

A special thank you and gratitude go to Trilogy Publishing for taking a chance on me and for their patience towards me while Jesus worked out all the details. I am forever grateful!

Table of Contents

Foreword

King David is described as a man after God's heart (1 Samuel 13:14; Acts 13:22). I think that description, a woman after God's heart, applies well to Susan. She loves Jesus with all her being and has sought to serve Him with the many gifts He has given her. Susan's devotions flow out of that love for Jesus and her God-given ability to use words to reflect His truth and love to others. She has wonderful insights and personal stories that connect with people and help draw them closer to Jesus. I am blessed to serve Jesus with Susan, and thank God this dream has become a reality.

—Pastor Robert Mrosko,
Brookfield Lutheran Church

> *"Strength and dignity are her clothing, and she laughs at the time to come" (Proverbs 31:25, ESV).*

I believe these words from King Solomon are true for Susan. Susan is a kind and compassionate woman who regularly seeks to follow Jesus more closely. Her experience and passion for following Jesus are evident in her life as she daily seeks to live a life of faith.

—Rev. Eric Kolonich,
Brookfield Lutheran Church

Susan is a thoughtful, mission-minded writer as she points people to Jesus through her devotions. I am so impressed with her deep dive into the Word of God as she prepares her words to share. I continue to encourage Susan to share her wisdom and insight as she is inspired to serve others in the kingdom of God.

—Mary Stafford-Nunez,
Director of Missions and Leadership
Brookfield Lutheran Church

Susan Butcher has been a friend for all seasons, and I thank God for the over forty years we have done life together! She has been "iron sharpening my iron," always encouraging me with the truth of God's Word, a listening ear, and a heart that accepts me as I am.

I have found her to be an avid student of God's Word…a wordsmith…constantly seeking to relate His truth faithfully and practically. All of this flows from a heart that has personally experienced deep pain and the healing only God can provide. She understands the power of God's grace as well as His forgiving love and perfect acceptance. She truly walks her faith.

—Paula S.
Fellow Sister in Christ

I have known Susan for close to thirty years. I have found her to be a woman seeking after God's own heart, a faithful prayer warrior, a trusted and time-tested friend, teachable, and a teacher. I consider her a dear friend.

—P. S.

I have known Susan for many years—decades!—and have watched her meet challenges with courage and deep faith, always choosing to look up with trust and joy. She writes with wisdom and sensitivity born of experience and prayer. Her book is a 2 Corinthians 3:3 (ESV) manifestation of the way she lives—"a letter from Christ…written…with the Spirit of the living God…on tablets of human hearts."

—Marilyn H. Otto, JD
Fellow Sister in Christ

Introduction

This book came to fruition because of numerous encouragements to turn my blog into a devotional book. After much prayer and consideration, Jesus made it very clear to me that writing a book was the direction in which He was directing me to go. His hand has been evident throughout the writing process. It is a story all of its own.

This book is about my life—sharing of the many stories and God-sightings my Lord and Savior, Jesus Christ, has given me. I am, by nature, a storyteller. I love sharing stories to help others grow and change in their lives, but most of all, in their personal relationship with Jesus Christ. Each one of us travels through life on our own journey. Mine has taken me through some tough times, and I am not ashamed to share these with you in the hope that my lessons learned will be helpful and encouraging to you.

I have had a personal relationship with Jesus for many years. I have struggled some over the years, but through it all, Jesus Christ is the victor. He has never left me, never forsaken me, always encouraged me, and made His presence known. We are not guaranteed anything in life, but Jesus promises to be with us forever and a day.

This book was not written to be read as a yearly devotional but as one to be read whenever one needs encouragement. As you read this book, may the Lord Jesus Christ speak to you and the Holy Spirit touch your heart and help you discover more and more about Him, feeling His presence until you meet Him face to face. This is my prayer for you! God bless you on your journey!

Accountability

I am all about my personal accountability, but I don't always stand true to this. Many times in my life, I have thought I had fooled my friends, co-workers, acquaintances, Jesus, only to find out they knew all along what was going on. Silly me for trying to play a magician and focusing on a disappearing act with myself. Ugh.

During these stressful times in our world, I have been trying to evaluate and re-evaluate my position on life, where I stand on issues, where I have stood in the past, and what road I want to head down. The other day I was listening to a song by Johnathan Pierce. His song "What I Need Is You" struck a nerve within me. He sings that trying to fool everyone about who you are trying to be is tiresome. We can lose our joy and real hope. We get ourselves in messes. We try to hide our brokenness, sadness, and oft-times despair—all for trying to save face. We try to focus on everyone else's faults instead of our own. Romans 3:19–20 (ESV) says the whole world will be held accountable to God and that no human being will be justified because our sin is revealed to us. So, why not focus on this rather than ourselves? Then Matthew 12:36–37 (ESV) says that on the day of judgment, people will give account for every careless word they speak, for by our words, we will be judged, and by our words, we will be condemned. Again, surely this means those other than ourselves. Easy enough to focus on this.

However, Romans 14:12 (ESV) says, "So then, each of us will give an account of himself to God." Uh oh. This says I will have to give an account of myself and myself alone. Others' behavior, words, etc., are, quite frankly, none of my business but His. It is inappropriate for me to focus on anyone other than myself—quite convicting.

However, there is hope. Later in the song, he says that even though I can be a pretender and don't want to surrender to Him, He can and wants to fix my mess. He can make me whole and forgive my self-righteousness. I can't fool Him—He already knows and is waiting for me to realize all I need is Him. I don't need to be afraid of acceptance. Acceptance is mine through Jesus Christ. How comforting to be able to rest in this.

All these Scripture verses bring me back to my own personal accountability. Where do I stand today in this area? Do I believe what Scripture is saying, that accountability is black and white? There are no gray areas. Where do you stand? Food for thought…

Prayer

Dear Jesus,

Forgive me for those times I do not hold myself accountable in my walk with You. Accountability is in my quiet times in Scripture, my prayer life, the use of the gifts and abilities You have imparted to me, my relationships. I want to honor You in all that I do. Thank You for your grace and patience, and I continue to learn what it means to have a closer walk with You. Amen.

Reflection

____

____

____

____

____

____

____

Already Decided

In my early school years, I was not known as the best of listeners. My parents frequently heard during their parent-teacher conferences that I was well-liked and a good student but talked too much and didn't listen enough. Had you asked me at that time, I would not have agreed. However, my exuberance at being a talker and storyteller was in full force.

Unfortunately, this trait carried over into my teen years and somewhat into my adulthood. I had a problem with listening before I spoke. Still do, from time to time. I was enthusiastic about almost everything and would jump from one thing to another, without much thought, including decision making. Hopefully, over the years, I have gained more wisdom and knowledge.

A number of years ago, I was gung-ho about attending Bible school in England. I was a relatively new Christian at the time but just knew Jesus wanted me to do this. It was a wonderful idea. I had already made up my mind I was going. So, I took steps and made my plans. A wise friend asked me if I had consulted what Jesus had to say about this. I didn't answer. Then she asked a second and third time. "Hmmm," I said to myself, "I guess that might be a good idea."

I settled down and picked up my Bible. God led me to Isaiah 30:21 (ESV), which says, "And your ears shall hear a word behind you saying, 'This is the way, walk in it,' when you turn to the right or when you turn to the left." I must admit, that seemed like sound advice. I continued praying and reading Scripture for a few weeks when the Lord led me to Isaiah 55:8–9 (ESV). This says, "For my thoughts are not your thoughts, neither are your ways my ways, declares the Lord. For as the heavens are higher than the earth, so are my ways higher than your ways, and my thoughts than your thoughts." So, I guess I didn't know everything. Quite the concept! I am so thankful for my good friend, who was wise enough to call me out about what I was doing. Just because I thought attending Bible school was a good idea—certainly didn't mean Jesus thought it was. Although a grand idea, maybe not so much for me and my life.

I learned a valuable lesson during this time. What was it? To quit jumping ahead of Jesus and sit back, pray, read Scripture, seek counsel and *listen*. I no longer make hasty decisions or am "already decided" on a matter. Now I pray and seek out Scripture and the counsel of trusted friends. Psalm 46:10 (ESV) says, "Be still, and know that I am God." Now I do what Jesus expects me to do, seek Him first and know that He is God.

Oh, by the way, I did eventually go to Bible school. And *yes*, I am still quite the storyteller. I am even a much better listener. My teachers would be proud.

Prayer

Dear Jesus,

Please forgive me for jumping ahead of the Holy Spirit and You when I get ants in my pants about doing something. Help me continue to learn to sit back and be quiet, listening for that still small voice of You. Amen.

Reflection

____

____

____

____

____

____

____

Brand New Life

Have you ever thought about what life would have been like for you had you been born at another time, or as another person, or to another family? I know I did. I looked around at other families and wished they were mine. I wished I was a child of another family so I could benefit from their closeness. I wished I had been adopted. However, wishing did not make it happen.

In my very early twenties, the Holy Spirit called me into the saving knowledge of Jesus Christ. I was naïve in my understanding of what that meant. Actually, I didn't have a clue. All I knew was I was hoping to get to a better place in life from where I was. I devoured the Bible, listened to others' life stories and what Jesus was doing in their lives, went to Bible studies, memorized scripture, talked to others about my own faith, and went to church. I heard consistently that God was my Father. However, I struggled with this concept. I just wasn't able to see Him that way because of my own relationship with my earthly father. We had no relationship, and I never felt loved by him, so how could God love me if he was my Father? It wasn't until the relationship with my human father began to change did I understand this fully. I had been given a new life, a new Father, and a family.

First Peter 1:3 (ESV) says, "According to his great mercy, he has caused us to be born again to a living hope through the resurrection of Jesus Christ from the dead." I was born again! I had been given a new life and everything to live for, including a future in heaven. I also had a new Father! Romans 8:15–16 (ESV) says that I had been adopted by Jesus Christ and was now able to call Him Abba Father. His Spirit bore witness to me that I was now one of His children and an heir of His future for me! I also received a new church family, one concerned about my spiritual growth, one that assisted me in walking the straight and narrow in my faith, one that prayed for me, counseled me, and encouraged me. A church family that still does. All this is because the Holy Spirit called me and of what Jesus Christ has done for me. My wish had come true.

First Peter 1:6 (ESV) states that no matter what may happen and the trials I may grieve along the way (so that my faith may be purified), all are meant to bring glory and praise to Him. The outcome of my faith is the salvation of my soul and life eternally with my Savior and Lord, Jesus Christ.

Do you wish that your life could be different, with a different family, different friends, different church? Do you long to know what the future will bring? Put your trust in Jesus Christ. He will give you a new life. He will give you a new hope, not a hope based on what we can see, but a hope based on truth (Scripture) and His promises that will never fail. *And* a future of life, eternally with Him. He has never let me down, and He will never let you down.

Prayer

Dear Jesus,

I long for a better life, more stability, more support from family and friends, and a future that is sure. I know I can only obtain this with You. Help me rest and rely on You and strongly walk out my faith and give all the praise and glory to You.

Reflection

____

____

____

____

____

____

____

Chains

I don't know about you, but I love jewelry. I mean, I really *love* jewelry. I have a number of items that have been given to me or that I have bought over the years that were expensive. However, I usually don't spend much money on it because I am one of those people who bore easily. When this happens, I have been known to give it away. Now, every once in a while, I come across something that I want the moment I see it. This happened one day, several years ago, when I was perusing Amazon. It was a handcuff bracelet. Yes, you read that correctly.

You may be thinking and saying to yourself, "Why in the world would she want that?" I have an answer to that question. You see, for a number of years, I had the privilege of being employed within the Department of Corrections. I served as a chaplain at a women's prison and worked with at-risk, underprivileged young adults and their families. I also was employed as a teacher at an adult prison in my hometown. I chose not to look at those I worked with as criminals but as those whom Jesus died for. The Word of God and salvation are for them, too.

Apostle Paul says that he suffered and was bound with chains as a criminal. He goes on to say, in 2 Timothy 2:9–10 (ESV), that although he was bound in chains, "the word of God is not bound! Therefore, I endure everything for the sake of the elect that they may obtain the salvation that is in Christ Jesus with eternal glory." You see, my bracelet reminds me that I am no longer in chains because of what He has done for me. I knew this was also true for those I worked with.

I look for things I can use to share my faith: books, bookmarks, cards, small gifts, coffee mugs, and other things, including jewelry. I am proud to wear this bracelet, which has a deep double meaning to me. People ask me why I wear it. I love being able to talk about my Lord and Savior, Jesus Christ, using things people don't expect. Would you consider doing the same?

If you do, I believe you will find open doors and great joy in sharing your faith using the unusual. Remember, you are no longer bound by chains, but you have been set free by the death and resurrection of Jesus Christ. Rejoice and be glad in it.

Prayer

Dear Jesus,

Thank You for Your death on the cross for me and the knowledge that I am no longer in chains. I have been set free from my past, forgiven for my sins, and now have the guarantee of eternal life with You. Please let me never forget that and always be thankful. Amen.

Reflection

____

____

____

____

____

____

____

Challenge, Prayer, and Fire

Daniel was quite the man. Scripture says he "became distinguished above all other presidents and satraps, because an excellent spirit was within him. And the king planned to set him over the whole kingdom" (Daniel 6:3, ESV). A satrap is a president, a governor, a ruler, an official. Daniel was above all these, and all others became his adversaries. They fought against Daniel's high morals, his integrity, and his commitment to the God of Israel. His enemies were angry, and they set out to get him.

In the satrap's evaluation of Daniel, they could find nothing wrong with him. So they set out to find a problem with his connection with God (Daniel 6:5, ESV). What they did was to "establish an ordinance and enforce an injunction that stated that anyone who makes a petition to any god or man other than the king would be cast into the den of lions" (Daniel 6:7, ESV). They talked with the king and had him sign the document, knowing full well what Daniel would do.

When Daniel heard of this, without hesitation, he *immediately* went to his house, where he had windows in his upper room open toward Jerusalem. He got down on his knees *three times a day and prayed, giving thanks before his God, as he had always done*.

Daniel's adversaries saw what Daniel was doing and tattled to the king, reminding him of the petition he signed. The king had no choice but to have Daniel thrown into the lion's den (Daniel 6:10–12, ESV). The thugs were overjoyed; the king was not. The king was heartbroken and labored without sleep, saying to Daniel, "May your God, whom you serve continually, deliver you" (Daniel 6:16, ESV). Daniel was thrown in with the lions, and the stone was laid at the mouth of the den. There was no escape.

Or so it seemed. The next morning, the king ran to the den and called out to Daniel and shouted, "Has your God...been able to deliver you from the lions?" Imagine the shock on the faces of Daniel's adversaries when Daniel said *yes!* Daniel told the king that the Lord had sent an angel to shut the mouths of the lions, and he was unharmed. The king was ecstatic and immediately had Daniel's adversaries and everyone in their families destroyed. The lion's den was a victory for Daniel. It was the end of the story for his enemies.

The moral of this story? Do what you know you should do even when you know you could be punished. How? By losing friends, losing a job, losing status, maybe losing your life. You see, God knows what His plan is. We may only see a negative one. Daniel was not afraid to pray and worship *his* God, even at the possible expense of his life. God had a different plan than what appeared to be. Again, do what you should do and allow God to continue to work out His plan, even when all seems lost.

By the way, Daniel prospered, the king was overjoyed, and God was honored and glorified. Are you open to having an excellent spirit? Are you willing to do what you know you should do, despite the consequences? Are you willing to be a Daniel?

Prayer

Dear Jesus,

Please forgive me for the times I don't do what I know I should do. My heart longs to be a Daniel, but my flesh is often weak. Help me to take a stand when I know I should so others will see, and You will be glorified. I want to be willing to be a Daniel. Amen.

Reflections

____

____

____

____

____

____

____

Challenges

Each new year brings with it, for me, a time of self-evaluation and goal setting. As I have evaluated each year, I usually find I am not happy with some areas. Unfortunately, it is almost always the area of my spiritual growth and walk with Jesus. I have found myself trying to fool my closest friends, loved ones, myself, and Jesus. How silly, trying to fool Jesus or anyone for that matter. I am only fooling myself. I imagine Him looking at me and saying, "Now, Susan (me), what are you doing?"

Over the past year, I have been broken and have sometimes briefly lost my hope and joy. Life brings hardships and challenges. How we face these makes all the difference between a life of anger, resentment, weariness, fear, *or* thankfulness, joy, and a realization that Jesus is in control and nothing touches us except those things that have passed through His nail-scarred hands. Among everything else, Jesus can fix the messes I find myself in. I learned a long time ago that I don't need a miracle for me to believe He is there and to experience His power.

My goal for each year is to come to a more comprehensive vision of Jesus, who He is, and what He has in store for me. Quite the challenge, right? To accomplish this means, for me, to surrender to Him, ask for help, marvel at His faithfulness, and stand firm in who I know He is. I am looking forward to this, knowing that all I need is Jesus.

Hebrews 12:1 (ESV) says, "Let us also lay aside every weight, and sin which clings so closely, and let us run with endurance the race that is set before us." So, I run on to the task ahead…knowing that with Jesus, the race is already won.

Prayer

Dear Jesus,

You know that I don't like to run. But You have asked me to run life's race, with endurance, so that I may win the prize. Help me keep at it.

Reflection

____

____

____

____

____

____

____

Change

Some people do well with change, and some don't. What is the difference between those who can handle change and those who can't? In my opinion, it simply comes down to what we value. Some of us value our own ambition and self-preservation more than Jesus' mission. If personal comfort is our main goal in life, we will fight against change. However, if Jesus is our ultimate treasure, change becomes an exciting opportunity. In Acts 6 (ESV), the apostles made a tough leadership decision while gathering together that affected lots of people.

The apostles realized that without a drastic change, the Gospel would not reach the world. They felt they had to serve tables rather than preach—preaching was their gift and their calling. So, they appointed seven men to take on the duty of serving tables. They needed to change something in order to be able to fulfill their mission. What happened when they did this? Because the early church was willing to change, "a large number of priests became obedient to the faith" (Acts 6:7, ESV).

When change faces us, we get to decide what kind of person we are going to be and evaluate what we treasure in life. Will we embrace change positively and allow growth to happen?

Imagine what would transpire in your walk with Jesus if you opened your heart to change. Imagine what would happen in our churches if we were willing to make the changes necessary to have more and more people hear the Gospel of Jesus Christ. What do you think Jesus would think about that?

My question to you is, are you willing to do whatever it takes to change your life when He asks? What would the result be if you did? How different would your life be? Something serious to think about.

Prayer

Dear Jesus,

You know change is not easy for me. However, because You want me to grow in my relationship with You, I must change. Help me to be faithful in this. Amen.

Reflection

____

____

____

____

____

____

____

Clay

There is a pottery studio close to where I live, so from time to time, I enjoy going there, being quiet, and being creative. Because I am able to go there early in the morning, there usually is no one except the person working there and me. I take my time picking out something to paint and the colors I will use. I know I will be there a while and have time to think.

The last time I visited this studio, I was silently praying as I worked, and this scripture came to mind, "He drew me up from the pit of destruction, out of the miry clay, and set my feet upon a rock, making my steps secure" (Psalm 40:2, ESV). I thought about the words "miry clay." He took me up from the miry clay, from a thick mud or a troublesome situation. For me, He rose me up from both. Before I made a personal commitment to Him, my life was as muddy as it could be, and I was in a dire, troublesome situation. Enough so that I could not see my way out of it.

So, here I was, working with clay and trying to make

something beautiful out of it. It fell apart again and again as I tried to work out my design with this lump of clay. The young lady working there came to help me from time to time, taking my lump of clay and making it solid and secure.

Isn't that what He does for us? He takes our lives, lifts us up, insecurities and everything, sets our feet upon a rock (Him), and makes our steps secure. As I looked back on my life that day (and many other times), I saw His hand and how He rescued me when I saw no way out. He took something ugly (my life) and made something beautiful out of it (only because of what He has done for me).

I went home that day with a beautiful coffee mug. Each time I use it, I think about all He has done for me. Without Him, I would be nothing. But with Him, I am safe and secure. Praise the Lord!

Prayer

Dear Jesus,

Thank You for taking me from the miry clay and placing my life on solid ground. Thank You that I am safe and secure in You. Please help me always remember Your saving grace and Your rescue from the pit—how I praise You!

Reflection

____

____

____

____

____

____

____

Did I Say That?

Have you ever looked back on the past to consider something you did or said and couldn't believe it? But yet, there it was, in black and white. Sometimes I do that with my writing. Some days I struggle with thoughts like, *I have nothing to say to others*; *Who would read my thoughts? Am I really doing what Jesus has called me to do?* Fear, fear, fear.

Today I came across something I wrote about two years ago. Funny how I still seem to struggle with the same areas in my life all the time. My foolishness, my frame of mind, my arrogance, my temporary loss of passion for the things Jesus has called me to do. Here are the words I wrote then…perhaps you are feeling somewhat the same as me?

> *When my hands, soul, and heart are tired of trusting those who let me down, Jesus, I give You everything. When I see what a hypocrite I am, how lost I feel, and I fail to go in the direction You have called me to, please bring*

> *me down to where I need to be...at Your feet. Take all my passion for temporal things and all my lies about who I think I am because I never knew what freedom was until you rescued me from the prison I was in. I'll keep on because, without You, there is no rhythm or reason to life.*

The Bible says the fear of the Lord is the beginning of wisdom. Not the kind of fear I am feeling with acceptance from others but the awe of knowing Him more and more each day.

So, today, I am going to do my best to rise above these things I am feeling about my life *again*! And follow Proverbs 1:7 (ESV), which says, "The fear of the Lord is the beginning of knowledge; fools despise wisdom and instruction."

Prayer

Dear Jesus,

I don't want to be a fool despite Your truth and instruction. I know my worth in You, and I want to cling to that. Thank You for Your grace and patience as I work on these areas of my life.

Reflection

____

____

____

____

____

____

____

Does He?

Does He? Does Jesus really care or understand? Has your mind ever gone down this road? Where did it lead you? I know I have, way too often. Allow me to share a story with you…

Let me begin this way. There have been questioning times in my life when this question has come to the forefront of my mind. How about you? It nags and nags at me until I start feeling guilty. Then I feel guilty that I feel guilty and am questioning. What a wild merry-go-round!

Several years ago, I went through this game (if I dare call it that). This was at a time when I wondered how my rent would be paid because of a massive amount of unexpected expenses. First, I was mad. Then anxiousness and fearfulness set in. *Then*, I decided to take it before the Lord. Why do I generally take it to the Lord as a last resort? A big hmmm…

At that time, I had a part-time job valet parking at a local hospital. You would think that tips would be good—not the case. One day I picked up a car to deliver it to its owner. She had a Christian radio station on. I love it when it happens. She pressed some money into my palm and told me to have a blessed day. When I looked, she had given me a twenty-dollar bill. She had no idea of my situation.

The next day I delivered yet another car to its owner and again had money put in my palm, all folded up. I shoved it in my pocket because I was busy. When I had a chance to look at it, it was a hundred-dollar bill. I was shocked. I asked someone if it was real and, yes, it was. I didn't take it to the bank to deposit for several days because I kept expecting her to come back and claim it. Really, Susan (that's me)? Shame on me. I had forgotten to say, "Thank You, Jesus!" Will I ever learn?

Psalm 8:4 (ESV) and Hebrews 2:6–9 (ESV) ask the question about who man is that He should care for us. Yet, He has crowned us with glory and honor when we are children of His. So, does He know and care about our every need? You betcha. Did my rent get paid? You betcha!

Why are you holding back thanking Him? Perhaps because He has not answered your situation (whatever that may be) yet? Or He has answered, and you have ignored having a thankful, grateful heart. We all need to be cognizant of where our hearts are and not forget where everything we have comes from, Him. I am working on this. Will you, too?

Prayer

Dear Jesus,

Sometimes I am so ungrateful for what You provide. How can I be? I know everything comes from You, including the surprises You bestow on me. Help me to be quick to always thank You.

Reflections

____

____

____

____

____

____

____

Dry Bones

Dry bones. What a concept. Have you ever thought about this? In Ezekiel 37:1–14 (ESV), Ezekiel had a vision in the middle of a valley full of very dry bones. He took his vision before God and asked about what it meant. God told him to prophesy over the bones and say to them,

> *Hear the word of the Lord. Thus says the Lord God to these bones: Behold, I will cause breath to enter you, and you shall live. And I will lay sinews upon you, and will cause flesh to come upon you, and cover you with skin, and put breath in you, and you shall live, and you will know that I am the Lord.*
>
> **Ezekiel 37:4–6 (ESV)**

So, Ezekiel followed orders. And, what happened? He heard a tremendous rattling, and the bones began coming together. As he looked up, breath and flesh came into the bones, and they lived. The bones stood on their feet, and an exceedingly great army came about. Seems impossible?

There was a time in my life when I was nothing but

dry bones. My life was in shambles. My heart was hard. My emotions were numb. Then the Holy Spirit's hand fell upon me. His working in my life started with a friend telling me that Jesus loved me. I questioned that. How could a loving God love me? Did He know where I was and where I had been? Surely, God could never love such a person as I. As the Holy Spirit continued to work, I began feeling my dry bones shake. God was beginning to move me. I sensed I was going from death to life. I realized that just as He was resurrected, my life could be too. If He rose from the dead, there was nothing He could not do, including giving life to my dead soul.

How about you? Are you still dry bones? You don't have to be. Call out to Him, and He will give your dry bones and dead heart new life (Psalm 40:3, ESV). He will restore your "dead man walking" to walking alive and victoriously with Him. He is able to deliver and save. He is able to help you walk again. With God, all things are possible (Matthew 19:26, ESV). Just ask me.

Prayer

Dear Jesus,

Thank You that once my bones were "dry bones" but now are not. Thank You that through You, my dry bones have been resurrected into a new life with You. Thank You for delivering and saving me. Thank You for helping me walk again. All praise goes to You! Amen.

Reflection

Fog

"Now we see only a dim likeness of things. It is as if we were seeing them in a foggy mirror. But someday we will see clearly" (1 Corinthians 13:12, NIRV).

Have you ever wondered if God knows what He is doing? Ever questioned Him? I know I have, especially during the trying times of my life. Sometimes I don't understand His wisdom, His timing, His anything. I question what He wants me to do, where He wants me to go, who He wants me to talk to, why my prayers don't seem to be answered, etc., etc., etc. Is this the way it is supposed to be?

The other day I was driving to my gym very early in the morning (I mean very early, like 5:30 a.m.). I rolled out of bed, brushed my teeth, and headed out. My brain was still a bit foggy. Once I drove out of my garage, I looked out into what I thought would be sunlight. However, I could not see across the street; I could not see beyond the fifty feet in front of my face. It was a bit frightening. Everything was in a deep fog. It brought to mind the above scripture.

At times I feel like I am in a fog, not able to see much of anything. The rest of the above verse says, "Now I know in part; then I shall know fully, even as I have been fully known" (1 Corinthians 13:12, ESV). God's plan for ultimate salvation is not seen clearly now but will be very clear in eternity. He is all-knowing, and someday, we will share His ultimate plan with Him for eternity if we know Him here on earth.

Thank God for this, to know that I shall know and understand fully what His plan is/was for me! It may not be in my timing, but it sure is in His! No fear of the unseen. No more fog, but seeing clearly. There is hope in this. How grateful I am. How about you?

Prayer

Dear Jesus,

How I long to know Your ultimate plan for me and for all eternity. Please forgive me when I become impatient with Your plan and want to know it right now. Amen.

Reflection

Freedom

Freedom. A strong word, meaning several things. My favorite ones are "the state of not being enslaved or imprisoned" and "the liberation from slavery or restraint or from the power of another." So, how does this apply to Christians? I did a study on how the Bible looks at freedom, our freedom. Here is what it says.

John 8:36 (ESV) says, "So if the Son sets you free, you will be free indeed." Romans 6:22 (ESV) and Romans 8:2 (ESV) say, "But now that you have been set free from sin and have become slaves of God, the fruit you get leads to sanctification and its end, eternal life": "For the law of the Spirit of life has set you free in Christ Jesus from the law of sin and death." Galatians 5:1 (ESV) says, "For freedom Christ has set us free; stand firm therefore, and do not submit again to a yoke of slavery." And last, 1 Peter 2:16 (ESV) says, "Live as people who are free, not using your freedom as a cover-up for evil, but living as servants of God."

Biblical freedom is freedom of the heart and mind, being free from earthly desires and passions. This does not mean that we do not struggle with earthly things. After all, we are human beings and are constantly bombarded by worldly things and temptations. We are all sinners saved by grace. Our freedom comes from knowing Jesus and His ways. Psalm 119:45 (ESV) says, "I will walk about in freedom, for I have sought out your precepts." If we know Jesus, we can be liberated from slavery to sin. There is a vast difference between knowing facts about Jesus and actually knowing the unique person and the saving work of the Lord Jesus Christ. We are set free by grace through faith in the Son of God and what He accomplished on the cross when we belong to Him.

During my time working at a prison, I had the opportunity to meet many who were caught in the slavery of their pasts. They saw no way out. They had little, if any, hope for their future. I had the wonderful opportunity to share with my students the grace of my Lord Jesus Christ and what it could mean for them. Some caught on and experienced the joy only Jesus can give. For most, it didn't seem to make a difference.

We all desire freedom, whether it be from a particular sin, self-indulgence, substance abuse, etc. Jesus came to free us from sin, death, and everything that ensnares us. We need to start by acknowledging our brokenness and that we are slaves to sin. If we choose Jesus and follow Him daily, He will break the bonds of slavery, and we'll experience true freedom.

"So if the Son sets you free, you will be free indeed." Amen to that.

Prayer

Dear Jesus,

I long for freedom from sin and slavery. I know that true freedom only comes from You. Help me get to know You better and better each day and cling to You as my freedom. Amen.

Reflection

Grace

I don't know about you, but I love gifts. Not just receiving (although that is quite wonderful), but for me, my joy comes in also giving gifts. When I was a child, I was taught that one must earn a gift and that when attained, a return gift must be given to the person you received it from. In short, my belief system when younger was that if I didn't earn it, I didn't want it. It seemed like too much work and very unrewarding.

Advance to my adult years… This philosophy was still part of my belief structure. I could not imagine (and still struggle some with this) that someone would freely give me a gift without there being a "payback" involved. *That can't be right or possible*, I thought. This thought pattern carried over to the time Jesus was working in my unsaved heart. Someone shared with me, as I struggled with this concept, the verse Titus 3:7 (ESV), which says, "So that being justified by his grace we might become heirs according to the hope of eternal life." I knew I needed some time to contemplate this. Several weeks later, I spoke with this person again. This time, she shared Ephesians 2:8–9 (ESV, emphasis added), which says, "For by grace you have been saved through faith. And it is not your own doing; it is the *gift* of God, not a *result of works*, so that no one may boast."

Could it possibly be that God wanted to give me a gift, the precious gift of salvation through Jesus Christ, without my having to first earn it and return it? Mind blown! If I accepted this as Scripture says, my entire gift receiving and giving frame of mind would have had to change. Was I ready for this? Would I believe it? So, I decided to give it a try.

Needless to say, I knew I had a lot of work to do, to know that not everyone who gives a gift expects one in return. Needless to say, I have never been sorry I took that chance. I have experienced God's never-ending grace upon grace in my life. He has shown me the immeasurable riches of His grace in kindness towards me in Jesus Christ (Ephesians 2:7, ESV), a gift freely given by His sacrifice on the cross for me. A gift accepted and never taken for granted.

Have you become an heir justified by grace, and do you have the hope of glory and eternal life with Him? My hope is that you do. If not, check out what He has to say to you, as I did. I promise you will never be sorry.

Prayer

Dear Jesus,

Thank You for Your immeasurable kindness and grace towards me. Despite the fact that I know I frequently let You down, You still have offered me Your free gift of salvation and eternal life. Help me to never take this for granted. Amen.

Reflection

____

____

____

____

____

____

____

He Is for Us

Sometimes I am overwhelmed by life's circumstances and just plain too tired to walk the walk, much less run the race set before me. Discouragement sets in. My mind wanders, sometimes thinking this Christian life and walk is just too hard. I want out, or at least a break. Sometimes I don't feel I am His; not a good place to be. However, this is not what Jesus Christ wants from you or me.

Music is a big part of my life, always has been, and I believe always will be. It has carried me through the most difficult times of my life, from childhood until now. So, when I find myself in the above state of mind, I challenge myself to read my Bible and listen to some music. One song I listen to a lot is "He Believes in You" by Danny Gokey. He sings about discouragement and pain setting into our lives and that we need to turn to Him, who is our hope. One line that I love so much states that He wouldn't put me through a fire unless He takes me higher. What a promise, one that is true and one that we can rest in. What an encouragement it is to *know* this, even if we don't *feel* it.

During these challenging times in my life, one of my favorite scriptures to turn to is Romans 8:31–32 (ESV). Here, it says, "What then shall we say to these things? If God is for us, who can be against us? He who did not spare his own Son but gave him up for us all, how will he not also with him graciously give us all things?" *If He is for us, who can be against us?* All right, okay. I get it and am reminded yet again. I have no excuse to feel sorry for myself or wallow in my discouragement. He knows and understands our trials, whether placed by Him or the result of living in a fallen world—His plan is to take us through the fire and set our feet on higher ground. Our hope can be alive because He is living inside of us. Will you remember this when your life seems to hit the fan? Will you go to your Bible to see what He has to say to you and perhaps listen to some Christian music to see what might be there for you? I pray you will.

Prayer

Dear Jesus,

Thank You for the knowledge that if You are for me, nothing or no one can prevail against me. When things get tough, may Your Holy Spirit bring this to my heart and mind, and may I practice what I know to be true. Thank You!

Reflection

Idolatry

Webster's Dictionary defines idolatry as "the worship of idols, images, or anything made by hands or which is not God." Idolatry is of two kinds: the worship of images, statues, pictures, etc., made by hands, and the worship of the heavenly bodies, the sun, moon, and stars, or of demons, angels, men, and animals." In biblical terms, idolatry is the worship of anything other than God. Colossians 3:5 (ESV) links covetousness and idolatry—when we want something so much that we covet it. When we spend all our time and devotion to it, at all costs, that thing has become an idol. Galatians 5:20 (ESV) says that the works of the flesh are evident: idolatry is just one of the things listed that we, as believers in Jesus Christ, need to stay away from.

With all that being said… Uh oh… I am in trouble, at least some of the time. This has brought a thoughtful pause in my life as of late. Going back over the years, I have looked at my life to see what, if anything, took hold of me over my relationship with Jesus Christ, even for a brief time. Here are some of the things I came up with: security, control, job, family, money, singleness, education, travel. Now, none of these are serious as a whole but things we all think about and challenge ourselves over. Nothing wrong with that, right? Herein lies the problem: when they become an obsession. For me, security and control have been a big issue. For a good share of my life, I did not feel I had control over anything. So, I tried to control everything. It became an overriding problem for me. Once the Holy Spirit called me into a saving knowledge of Jesus Christ, I knew I had to give up control and find my security in Him if I wanted to live my life for Him.

How about you? Do you serve idols, maybe some of the same ones I find myself serving now and then? If we are all honest about it, we all fall into this category. We need to be very careful. Does Jesus want us to serve idols of any kind? I know that answer is a resounding *no*. If we deny we serve idols, take a look at 1 Corinthians 10:12 (NIV), which says, "So, if you think you are standing firm, be careful that you don't fall!" First Corinthians 10:13–14 (ESV) goes on to say, "No temptation has seized you except what is common to man. And God is faithful; He will not let you be tempted beyond what you can bear. But when you are tempted, he will also provide a way out so that you can stand up under it." Let's search out the things of God, practice them, and let the idols rest.

Prayer

Dear Jesus,

I ask Your forgiveness for the times I find myself worshipping anything or anyone other than You. Worshipping idols is outright sin and not what You desire for me. Through Your Holy Spirit, help me become more aware of my wrongdoing and to get quickly back on the right track. Amen.

Reflection

____

____

____

____

____

____

____

It's Not Fair!

The other day I was in the grocery store and heard a resounding "It's not fair!" I looked around to see if I could see what was going on, and sure enough, it was a young child yelling this to his mom. It seemed as though she was not allowing him to clear off a shelf and put the items in their cart. I silently laughed. It seemed funny to me at the time.

However, yesterday my pastor spoke on this very phrase. Even though it was the second time I heard this said in just several weeks, yesterday, I did not laugh. It hit home with a thud. I was not happy. Today, I have been giving much thought to why yesterday it was no longer funny.

Romans 11:33–34 (NIV) says, "Oh, the depth of the riches of the wisdom and knowledge of God! How unsearchable his judgments and his paths beyond tracing out! Who has known the mind of the Lord? Or who has been his counselor?" What is this saying?

There are times I think I know more than the Lord

does. Do you find yourself doing this too? I am quite sure this upsets Him and makes His heart hurt. It saddens me that I know I break His heart. So, why do I think I know more than Him? Why He continues to love me unconditionally, I will never fully comprehend, yet He does. His compassion and grace are new every morning; great is His faithfulness (Lamentations 3:22–24, ESV).

I wish I didn't sometimes forget that He is an all-knowing God, that His judgments and ways are unsearchable and inscrutable. I look back on my life, to those times I thought I knew better. I see clearly now that He knew better than I. No one and nothing is above His knowledge about us and what He wants for us. I remember hearing Corrie ten Boom say that our life is like a completed tapestry. We see all the loose threads and an unfinished product because we see from the underside. Jesus sees the finished product because He is looking down from above. We don't know what the finished product looks like; He does. So, knowing this, will I rest in the knowledge that He always knows better and stop screaming, "It's not fair!"? Will I let Him decide what is best, what is worst, and what is right? I don't know about you, but I want to work on this so that I please Him in my responses when I don't understand what He has brought across my path. Will you do this, too?

Prayer

Dear Jesus,

Forgive me for those times I feel I know more than You. How foolish of me. Please remind me when I do this that You are in control and that You are all-knowing. Amen.

Reflection

Keith Urban and Rhubarb Pie

One of the things most people don't know about me is that I was raised on rhubarb, rhubarb sauce, rhubarb pie, rhubarb muffins, rhubarb cake… You get my drift. I *love* rhubarb, especially pie. I don't know why, but over the years, people started adding strawberries to it. Strawberry rhubarb pie. Yuck!

Another thing some people don't know about me is that I love country music. Rascal Flatts is my favorite country group. Carrie Underwood and Keith Urban are among my favorite single acts.

Now, aren't you glad you have this intimate knowledge about me? I thought you might. Perhaps you are wondering or thinking, "Okay, where's she going with this?" Please allow me to unfold my story…

I am not so happy about ever having to be confined to my home, albeit I understand the importance at various times of having to do so, especially when I am sick. One day when I was not feeling well, I was feeling particularly antsy and unhappy about having to be at home. So, I prayed about it. I decided to check out Facebook, only to find that Keith Urban and his wife were doing a live Facebook concert from their home. I was ecstatic! Keith sang his new song, "God Whispered Your Name." It brought me back to the time when God whispered the name Jesus to me when I felt down and out. That whisper started a whole new life for me, one that included a personal relationship with God's Son. Now I was feeling better.

Right at the end of Keith's concert, there was a loud knock on my door. I opened it to find a neighbor standing there. He said, "We've bought pies for everyone," and handed me a bag with a pie in it. I didn't know what to say except thank you. I took my pie into the kitchen and decided to take a look at it. What I saw brought tears to my eyes. Guess what kind of pie it was? Go ahead, guess. Come on…guess! Yes, it was straight-up rhubarb pie with *no* strawberries!

Jesus provided me with two of my favorite things to enjoy that day. If we (you and I) just focus on who Jesus is and what He's done for us, He will bring your joy back to you. Maybe not Keith Urban or rhubarb pie, but something that will help you focus on the good things He has done for you. Luke 12:32 (ESV) says, "Fear not, little flock, for it is your Father's good pleasure to give you the kingdom." Notice this verse is in the past and present tense. What do I mean? First, it means that He has already given us the kingdom. Second, all we need to do is wait for Him to implement it into our lives. He *has already* given us the kingdom when we belong to Him. I experienced it that day. I asked for nothing, yet He gave me blessings!

So, this is the end of my story, at least for now. So, I will say goodbye and go find another piece of rhubarb pie.

Prayer

Dear Jesus,

Thank You for giving even when I don't deserve it and am ungrateful for it. Thank You for already giving me the kingdom. May I never forget that. Amen.

Reflection

____

____

____

____

____

____

____

Lawful versus Helpful

Having morals, character, and ethical behavior can be difficult, to say the least. Sometimes it means going against the flow, being different than our friends, taking personal responsibility, and not accepting what the world and society have to say about dignity and integrity. Sometimes it just seems easier to take a stand in our hearts than by what comes out of our mouths. After all, if we don't take a stand, then no one will know where we stand. Right?

However, the Bible is very clear about how our conscience should predict our behavior. I remember when I was a child saying to my parents, "But everyone is doing it." My parents simply replied, "Well, that doesn't make it right." I always tried my best to instill this within the minds of the male prisoners I worked with. At the prison, I frequently heard, "I didn't get caught." Okay. My reply was, "Did you break the law?"

"Yep, but I didn't get caught."

"You still broke the law, and that is not right," I all too

often replied. "Just because you didn't get caught doesn't make it right. Own up to what your heart is telling you is right and wrong!"

First Corinthians 6:12 (NIV) says, "'Everything is permissible'—but not everything is beneficial. 'Everything is permissible'—but not everything is constructive." The English Standard Version (ESV) says, "'All things are lawful for me,' but not all things are helpful." And concludes by saying, "but not all things build up."

As we look at our lives and our relationship with Jesus Christ, what are our goals? Is it to blend in with others? Is it to look at ourselves and evaluate the things that are holding us down, holding us back from moving forward? Or is our witness confusing and bringing others down? Is our attitude, "Okay, I am saved, so I can do anything and everything I want"? "Does it really matter if I don't get caught?" I sincerely hope not. It is difficult to take a stand when the world tells us it is okay if we don't. All things may be lawful, but are they helpful? All things may be lawful, but do they build others up?

I want to be the kind of Christian who takes a stand, not obnoxiously but firmly, on those things that matter to my Lord and Savior, Jesus Christ. I would love to say I do this all the time, but I do not. I am a work in progress. My goal is to honor Him, all the while standing up for those things that bring Him dishonor and sadness to His heart. How about you?

Prayer

Dear Jesus,

Just because everyone else is doing it doesn't fly. You call us to be obedient to what we know in our hearts to be true. Please forgive me when I don't follow this.

Reflection

Life Verse

I recently heard the phrase "prepare the day for us and prepare us for the day" as a prayer and a wonderful way to start one's day. I thought that was a wonderful idea and decided I would start doing that. Weeks have passed. So, have I done this? *No*! For me, not doing so is two-fold: *changing* the focus from myself to Him first and *making the conscious decision* to "just do it."

When change is needed, we get to decide what kind of person we're going to be and what we value. Will we embrace change positively and allow growth to happen? This is a wonderful, useful question and one that I have considered frequently.

With Jesus Christ, our lives are different and changing every day if we allow it. The question is, do I want to be growing and different in my walk with Him? Sometimes I wonder. My life verse is Psalm 40:8 (ESV), "I desire to do your will, O my God; your law is within my heart." Sometimes I get side-tracked and forget this. Sometimes I am all talk and no action. Action words in my walk with

Him are trust, delight, commit, pray. Decisive, prayerful action on my part is what is needed for Him to have His way in me and work out what He wants for me.

If I would just delight myself in Him before my day starts, I wonder how different my days would be and how different a person I would become.

How about you?

Prayer

Dear Jesus,

So often, I neglect asking You to be with me throughout my day. I don't pray. I don't have my quiet time. I just go about my business. Please forgive me for the times when I do this and help me refocus to make You the center of my day. Amen.

Reflection

____

____

____

____

____

____

____

Loose Threads

Years ago, I had the privilege of hearing Corrie ten Boom speak at my church. She and her family were arrested for hiding Dutch Jews during the war. They were sent to concentration camps. Although she survived, all ten members of her family died in the camps. At church that day, she spoke of God's preservation of her and her sister through the worst of life, battling illness, depression, and loneliness. Her sister was the last to die, leaving Corrie alone in the camp. Twelve days after her sister's death, she was released from the camps for reasons unknown to her at the time. She then moved back to the Netherlands after the war and started her ministry, taking in those who had helped the Germans. In 1977, she moved to California.

She did not come to immediately realize God's purpose for her life. In her travels and speaking engagements, she came upon the German soldier who was the worst of the worst at her camp. She had just finished giving a talk on forgiveness when she saw him. She found herself frozen when he extended his hand to shake hers. He did not recognize her. As they spoke, he told her he had come to a saving knowledge of Jesus Christ over the years.

Ms. ten Boom often told a story of life being like a tapestry. You see, we see the underside because we are looking up at it; there seems to be no rhyme or reason for what we see. There are loose threads, hanging and going every which way, and knots; it is a totally unfinished product. However, God sees it as the finished product of a gold jeweled crown because He sees it looking down. This same crown is waiting for us if we belong to Him (1 Peter 5:4, ESV).

Are there things in your life you don't understand? Circumstances and situations that baffle you? Isaiah 55:8–9 (ESV) says, "For my thoughts are not your thoughts, neither are your ways my, declares the Lord. For as the heavens are higher than the earth, so are my ways higher than your ways, and my thoughts than your thoughts." Are you focusing on the hanging threads and not the finished tapestry? Just as Ms. ten Boom didn't see the final outcome, neither can we see it. We need to focus on the fact that God knows exactly what He is doing, even if we are not able to see or understand it. Let's work towards doing what we know we have been called to do and leave the rest up to Him.

Prayer

Dear Jesus,

Sometimes it seems like my life is a mess of tangles, knots, and loose threads. But I know that this mess will turn into a gold jeweled crown, waiting for me when I, at last, see You face to face.

Reflection

____

____

____

____

____

____

____

Martyr

Martyr. Interesting word. Not a word in my daily vocabulary. A word that I don't think much about, at least not until the past few weeks, when I needed to. You see, a friend of mine, who was a long-time missionary, died quickly after contracting a disease in the country where he and his wife were serving the Lord. A Christian martyr is someone who upholds the teachings of Jesus, basing everything they say and do on His Word. They are willing to die for what they are doing in the name of Christ. My friend was such a person.

My friend and his wife served as missionaries for thirty-plus years. They served without hesitation to the many risks and challenges they endured. They were unwavering in their faith and purpose to serve those God had given them to minister to. Their faith was enormous and unchanging. They hung on to and lived out 2 Corinthians 5:1–9 (NIV), which (in summary) says this,

> *For we know that if the earthly tent we live in is destroyed, we have a building from God, an*

> *eternal house in heaven, not built by human hands...Therefore we are always confident and know that as long as we are at home in the body we are away from the Lord. For we live by faith, not by sight. So we make it our goal to please him, whether we are at home in the body or away from it.*
>
> **2 Corinthians 5:1, 6–9 (NIV)**

Wow! What hope there is in Jesus. What confidence, knowing that we are only here temporarily and will be with Him eternally if we believe in Him as our Savior and Lord. There is a song called "Yes and Amen" by Chris Tomlin. The chorus says, in part, that all His promises are yes and amen.

I wonder and need to consider, am I living the way my friend did? Do I live life with an urgency and passion for sharing the Gospel so others too may rest in the knowledge they will have eternal life with Jesus Christ? Will I be able to say, as in 2 Timothy 4:7 (ESV), "I have fought the good fight, I have finished the race. I have kept the faith."? Am I willing to lose my life because of sharing the Gospel of Jesus Christ? I want to live my life as my friend did. I want to share the same eternal hope in Jesus Christ that he had and I have with others. How about you?

Prayer

Dear Jesus,

Thank You that You gave Your life for us so that we may have eternal hope and know that we will be sharing our eternity with You. Please give me a heart and passion for those who do not know You.

Reflection

My Victory

I was recently at my favorite coffee shop, drinking coffee, eating, and listening through my headset to my music library. It is a small place, the tables are close, and even though I often listen to music or a podcast, I am still able to hear what others are talking about. I usually try to tune it out, but this day something piqued my interest. So, I decided to carefully listen in. The conversation did not appear to be of a personal nature but one about God and Jesus. I had no intention of trying to join the conversation, albeit I would have liked to.

The people involved were discussing Jesus' death and resurrection and what it meant to them. It appeared that they knew it is said that Jesus died on a cross, but this fact didn't seem to hold any meaning for them. In fact, one of them made the comment, "So what?" That's a big "so what" in my book. They went on to discuss that "everyone does things that are not right," but for them, the fact was, "Who cares?" This didn't mean they were bad people, and surely they would go to heaven because they were good people, and they tried not to harm others. I wondered if they had considered how their words and actions affected others, not just themselves. Was their optimism about heaven misplaced? It seemed to me they were trusting in themselves for salvation, not trusting in the only one who can gift it.

Ironically (well, maybe not), I had been listening to a song by David Crowder called "My Victory" when I first heard them talking. My favorite thought from this song is that the cross that was meant to kill Jesus is my victory. Crowder goes on to sing that everything we have done and all that we are has been nailed into His hands on the cross. When we are believers in Jesus Christ (not just believers but truly walking with Him by praying, reading our Bible, going to church, being involved in some type of ministry), the cross is our victory. First John 5:4–5 (ESV) says, "For everyone who has been born of God overcomes the world. And this is the victory that has overcome the world—our faith. Who is it that overcomes the world except the one who believes that Jesus is the Son of God?" I count myself as one of those who are born of God and one who trusts in Him for my eternal life.

I walked away that day so very thankful that I am His and that the cross He bore is my victory. As for those people I was listening to? I didn't say anything, but I prayed for them that day and continue to pray as He leads me. My hope is that they will come to realize, as I have, that Jesus is their only hope for a life in eternity.

Prayer

Dear Jesus,

Thanks and praise to You that what You suffered on the cross is now my victory. Help me be sensitive to those around me who I know are only trusting in themselves for Your salvation. I want to be bold in sharing my life with You with others.

Reflection

____

____

____

____

____

____

____

No What Ifs

If you are anything like me, and I imagine I don't have bragging rights to this, you have asked yourself too many times to remember, "What if?" Our "what ifs" can span our past, present, and future. Here are some of these I have asked myself: What if I don't get the job? What if my past had not been as it was? What if life doesn't give me what I think I should have? What if my prayers are never answered? What if I never get married? What if I get sick? What if, what if, what if!

Moses, a great spiritual leader in the Old Testament, struggled with this. In Exodus 3 (ESV), God tells Moses that He is going to persuade Pharaoh to bring the Israelites out of Egypt. He tells Moses that Pharaoh and the elders would not listen to him and that He, God, would be with him all the way (Exodus 3:10–12, ESV). Now, you would think that Moses would be encouraged by this and rest in the fact that God was with him. His response: What if? (Exodus 4:1, ESV)

I recently read that if we replace our "what if" with

"even if," it will have a liberating effect on us. That's quite a spin—turning a negative into a positive. This takes our eyes off ourselves and onto our loving Savior. Even if the worse happens, He is still with us.

In Deuteronomy 31:6 (ESV), God says to Moses, "Be strong and courageous. Do not fear or be in dread of them, for it is the Lord your God who goes with you. He will not leave you or forsake you." As if that weren't enough, God repeats it, "It is the Lord who goes before you. He will be with you; he will not leave you or forsake you. Do not fear or be dismayed" (Deuteronomy 31:8, ESV).

With Jesus, there are no "what ifs." This is what Paul has to say about this, "Do not be anxious about anything, but in everything, by prayer and petition, with thanksgiving, present your requests to God" (Philippians 4:6, ESV). Jeremiah 29:11(ESV) says, "For I know the plans I have for you, declares the Lord, plans for wholeness and not for evil, to give you a future and a hope." God knows the plans He has for me; He knew my days before I was even born (Jeremiah 1:5, ESV). I need to trust Him fully and learn to walk with Him in faith, knowing that all things are in God's sight. He is unchanging. He knows all. And He knows all about you and me.

How about turning our "what ifs" to "even if"? Question: How would our lives be different if we all started living like that?

Prayer

Dear Jesus,

Help me to lean on You when I feel my "what ifs" coming on and turn them to "even ifs." Thank You that You know the plans You have for me, and I never need to doubt your grace and Your love for me.

Reflection

____

____

____

____

____

____

____

Object, Experience, and Hope

I recently heard this somewhere, a statement made by *John Piper*, "The *object* of hope is future. The *experience* of hope is present. And that present experience is powerful."

What does this mean, and is it true? Object, experience, and hope. I thought long and hard about a recent life situation of a dear friend of mine. She was recently diagnosed with breast cancer. My heart breaks. What do I say to her? Everything seems cliché. I pray constantly and talk with her frequently. So, how does this situation play into the object, experience, and hope?

I have looked at Piper's "object of hope" as being in the future tense. I guess it is. There are things I hope for, such as my friend's radiation treatment and success in the future. She is an object of hope for me. I pray for her continued care, even if it is only for today or tomorrow. I am hopeful that she will be completely healed, which she will be, either here on earth or in eternity. She and I both know this.

Piper states that the *experience* of this hope is present tense, meaning right now. And yes, I do believe that this is true, too. I am experiencing this hope right now for my friend, so it is in the present tense. And this present, hopeful experience is powerful when we believe in the power of Jesus Christ. My friend and I talk about hope in Jesus Christ and what it means to us.

Romans 8:24–25 (ESV) says, “Now hope that is seen is not hope. For who hopes for what he sees? But if we hope for what we do not see, we wait for it with patience.” And Hebrews 6:11 (ESV) states, “And we desire each of you to show the same earnestness to have the full assurance of hope until the end.”

What are you hoping for? Are you standing firm, knowing Him who loves you with everlasting love and knows your heart? We can hope for a lot of things here on earth, but is our eternal hope desiring to spend eternity with Him? If not, it’s never too late to come to Him. He is waiting.

Prayer

Dear Jesus,

How I long to put all my hope in You and not myself. I desire for You to be the object of hope that I experience now and for eternity. Help me to have the full assurance of hope in You until the end. Amen.

Reflection

____

____

____

____

____

____

____

Old Self

I think and talk a lot about my old self when I am sharing my faith with others, my old self meaning what I call my "BC" days, before Christ. I am, by nature, a storyteller, and I have quite the story to tell about my life before I came to a saving knowledge of Jesus Christ.

To make a long story short, I was raised in a challenging environment. What I mean by this is my house was filled with a lot of anger, rage, and wrath. Unfortunately, I inherited these things growing up. It wasn't until I was in my early twenties that I saw a need to begin working on these areas of my life. At that time, I was filled with anger, rage, obscene talk, and malice towards my family and the things that had happened to me in my young life. However, when my relationship with Jesus Christ became my life, I knew these things were not honoring Him. Colossians 3:7–10 (ESV) says,

> *In these you too once walked, when you were living in them. But now you must put them all away: anger, wrath, malice, slander and*

> *obscene talk from your mouth. Do not lie to one another, seeing that you have put off the old self, with its practices and have put on the new self...*
>
> **Colossians 3:7–10 (ESV)**

Was I slow to anger and have a great understanding, or do I have a hasty temper and exalt folly? (Proverbs 14:29, ESV) I had put off the old self and replaced it with the new self when the Holy Spirit called me to a saving knowledge of Jesus Christ. I found, with the Holy Spirit's help, I had to rid these things of my past life in order to know and draw closer to Him. I wanted to triumph in these areas. I learned He is slow to anger and mighty in power (Nahum 1:3, ESV) and that He is merciful and gracious, abounding in steadfast love and faithfulness (Psalm 86:15, ESV). I am to take on the image of my Creator. If I was serious about my relationship with Him, I knew I must hang on to these verses.

How are you doing in these areas? Are you hearing the footsteps of anger, rejection, and resentment? Are there other voices at war in your spirit? If so, are you grabbing hold of His abounding grace and patience? Are you working diligently to become like your Creator, taking on His image? Just like I did, will you do some soul searching to see if there is anything holding you back from a closer walk with Him?

Prayer

Dear Jesus,

Thank You for what You have brought me through, and forgive me for all those things I forget You have done by Your death on the cross. Help me be clear in my thinking about who I am before You so that I will be able to develop a closer walk with You. Amen.

Reflection

Pain and Loss

Over the years of my life, I have experienced much pain and loss through death and illness. I mourned the loss of my father, my mother, sister, numerous other family members and friends. Some of my best friends have lost their families and children through miscarriages, cancer, and incurable diseases. I also have experienced loss, and my friends have, too, through suicide. Mary, the mother of Jesus, lost her son through crucifixion. The disciples lost their best friend, Jesus.

We live in a fallen world. This means that loss and pain are inescapable for all of us. For those who have a personal relationship with our Savior Jesus Christ, we can rest in the hope of knowing that they are with their loving Savior, and we will see them again. Revelation 21:4 (ESV, hereinafter, brackets added by the author) says, "He [Jesus] will wipe away every tear from their eyes and death will be no more, neither shall there be mourning nor crying nor pain anymore, for the former things have passed away." What hope!

My deepest mourning has come for those whom I believe did not know Him. My heart of hearts hurts for me and for those who have lost others, knowing this hope is not there. I have attended funerals where this hope is lost. What can I say to those who are suffering at that time? I can't honestly say they will see their loved ones again. What comfort can I give them, knowing hope is not there?

This is poignant for me. I wonder why it takes situations such as pain and loss for me to get up and do something, such as sharing my faith. Why am I not doing this consistently with those around me? We never know what life will bring us each day. We don't know whether death will come to us or to someone we know. There is no guarantee we, or our friends, will be here for another day. God is in charge of that. Knowing this, what am I doing to make sure those around me know about Jesus and that there is hope, an eternal hope, for them?

I live with the hope that I will spend eternity with Jesus. Am I willing to tell others about eternity and that in eternity there will no longer be pain and suffering because of what He has done for us? I don't want to wait anymore to tell others. I want to commit myself to sharing His love. Will you consider doing the same before it's too late for some? I hope you will.

Prayer

Dear Jesus,

Help me, through Your Holy Spirit, to see the needs around me and to be willing to share Your saving grace with others before it's too late for them. I want my goal to be seeing others come to know You personally so I know they have hope for eternity and that I will once again see them. Amen.

Reflection

____

____

____

____

____

____

____

Perfect Peace

Have you ever experienced perfect peace? I'm not sure I believe I ever totally have. Peace, yes. Perfect peace, no. Just what is perfect peace? Does it mean the absence of troubles, conflict, noise, stress, and anxiety? It seems like I have never been able to escape these things. Once one goes away, another one rears its ugly head. Then, does it mean rest, silence, and serenity will never be mine? I hope not because I don't always have these things in my life either.

Doing some research, I came across a blog that said, "Perfect peace is being calm in one's heart while in the midst of all unavoidable disturbances, troubles, hard work, and noise. Real peace is not the state of rest one may enjoy in serene and silent surroundings without any disturbance or distractions."

Perfect peace is more than the absence of conflict. It is the combination of wholeness and completeness as a direct result of faith in Jesus Christ and His finished work on the cross. It is more than simply the absence of anxiety and stress. It is an *abiding* and *deep knowledge* of being loved and cared for by God, no matter what.

John 14:27 (ESV) states that this perfect peace is a gift from God ("Peace I leave you with, my peace I give you."). It is not a tangible, physical or visible gift ("Not as the world gives do I give it to you."). It is a gift far better than this. His perfect peace rests your heart and mind when the tough things of life hit ("Let not your hearts be troubled, neither let them be afraid.").

I learned a long time ago that either He is in control or He is not and that I need to act accordingly. Isaiah 26:3 (ESV) says, "You [Him] keep him [us] in perfect peace whose mind is stayed on You, because he [us] trusts in You." Believe this or don't. If you do, the peace that passes all understanding will be yours.

Prayer

Dear Jesus,

I long to experience that perfect peace You offer. Help me weed through the "stuff" in my life while always looking to You for peace of heart, mind, soul, and spirit. Amen.

Reflection

____

____

____

____

____

____

____

Raise Your Hand

Today, I have been listening to music, which is always a blessing to me. Some of the songs I have listened to caused me to look back over my life and see where I was and where I am today. Coming up from the ashes, where my life was filled with emptiness—truly He has lifted me up from the miry clay (Psalm 40:2, ESV)—to feeling that emptiness filled with Jesus Christ. I see that I have had a front-row seat to His faithfulness. He has always been there, even when I felt He wasn't. Psalm 8:4 (ESV) says, "What is man that You are mindful of him, and the Son of man that you care for him?" I don't know why He loves or cares for me, but it is a fact. I know I don't deserve it, yet all He has to offer is *always* available to me. How thankful I am and what peace it gives me to know, no matter what, He is there, and He is enough.

How about you? Have you experienced this peace that passes all understanding? Do you know what it means to be on Jesus Christ's side? To work for Him? First Corinthians 15:58 (ESV) says, "Therefore, my beloved brothers, be steadfast, immovable, always abounding in the work of the Lord, knowing that in the Lord Your labor is not in vain." Jesus will show up and show off what He has done and what He has done for you.

Are you faithful to share His works and what He has done in your life with others? Are you grateful for all He has done for you? Do you realize that you can change the world with your words? Are you willing to take His side, no matter what?

You may not feel significant enough, worthy enough, strong enough. That is why Sunday's comin'! Raise your hand to that!

Prayer

Dear Jesus,

I will never understand why You chose to love me and die for me. I just know You did. You are always there for me and have never let me down. Help me to always remember that and that Sunday's comin'.

Reflection

Real Joy

A friend recently asked me if I thought I had lost my joy, I guess because life had been difficult for me for a while. I thought about it and replied, "No, not my joy, but perhaps a bit of my happiness." You see, happiness depends on my circumstances; joy depends on my relationship with Jesus Christ. I recently read an article in *Just Between Us* magazine. It spoke of kick-starting one's joy. Okay. So, how do I do that? Here's how… I can start out by being thankful and keeping a journal or thankfulness jar, where I place notes every day about what I am thankful for. I can pray—for others, for myself. This gets my eyes focused off my ingrown eyeballs. I can do something for someone else. I can find a creative outlet. Do what the psalmist suggests in Psalm 119:14 (ESV), and give constant praise for all He's done. First Thessalonians 5:16–18 (ESV) says to rejoice always, pray continually, and give thanks in all circumstances because this is God's will for us in Jesus Christ.

So, I have made a conscious decision to do this and

follow James 1:2–3 (ESV), which states, “Count it all joy, my brothers, when you meet trials of various kinds, for you know that the testing of your faith produces steadfastness.” So, I listen to music, sing out loud, listen to the Bible on YouVersion, tell others about what God is doing in my life, and pray (for my church, for others, for the world, and myself). I journal about what He is doing and has done in my life in the past and what He will do in the future, His goodness, grace, and faithfulness.

I marvel at His timing, making this article available to me at just the right time with its awesome suggestions. Is God real? Yes, He is. Does He care about our joy? Yes, He does. Happiness is fleeting; joy is not if we put our trust in Jesus Christ.

Prayer

Dear Jesus,

When life gets tough, I know I tend to have ingrown eyeballs, focusing on my life circumstances and not on You. Help me become more aware of when I begin doing this so that I may refocus on You and Your faithfulness, majesty, and glory. Amen.

Reflection

Rise Up

The other day several of my girlfriends and I were discussing the phrase "*rise up*" and what it meant to us. Initially, we all got a case of the giggles. Our thoughts were about how we would get up from the chairs we were sitting on after sitting on them for a few hours. Oh, my! There would probably be some rocking and rolling goin' on!

After our silliness, our thoughts turned to a more serious talk. Just what does "*rise up*" *mean*? I wanted to see what a dictionary and the Bible had to say about this. Here are a few things that came to light: to begin to exist, to originate, to come into being or notice; to be excited; to begin to move or act; to change a station, to leave a place, as to rise from a siege; to rise up to the battle (as in Jeremiah 49, ESV).

Luke 17:19 (ESV) says, "And he said to him, 'Rise up and go your way; your faith has made you well.'" Wow! What a commentary on my life. Before the Holy Spirit led me to understand who Jesus was and to know Him personally by committing my life to Him, I was in despair and saw no reason to carry on. When the Holy Spirit touched my life, I began to exist, to come into being. My station in life changed, and I left the place I was in. I rose up from a siege (a life full of sin and turmoil) and rose up to the battle. I rose up from my chair (a pun, here) to walk with Jesus. Has it been an easy rise? No. Has it been the best thing I have ever done? A resounding yes!

Do you find yourself fighting to rise up against something? Perhaps you don't know Jesus Christ personally. You can. Simply come before Him; acknowledge you are a sinner in need of being saved by grace. Ask Him to enter your life and accept His forgiveness.

Jesus is calling and saying, "Rise up and come with Me, to a new place, to begin to truly exist."

Prayer

Dear Jesus,

I want to know You personally, accept Your forgiveness, and experience the new life You have for me. Help me have the assurance I will live eternally with You.

Reflection

____

____

____

____

____

____

____

Separation

For many years I experienced separation anxiety. Not medically but emotionally. It seemed that I felt left out or separated by most everyone in my life. My parents divorced when I was fifteen years old, creating a situation where my friends left me because their parents would not allow them to associate with me; no one whose parents were divorced was good. My sister left home to get married. My friends left home to go to college. I was unable to make lasting friends at work for whatever reason. I felt distressed and alone. My difficult life situations had to be faced alone, or so I thought.

So, when a friend of mine began sharing with me about Jesus Christ and who He was, I laughed inside at her. She shared with me that I could be the victor in my life situations. She told me that because of Jesus' sufferings, my pain was a stepping stone to victory, eventually leading to living out my eternal life with Jesus Christ, who is the victor in and of all things.

The question she asked me was, did I know anyone

who could or would separate me from the love of Christ? She shared Romans 8:37–39 (ESV), which states, "No, in all these things we are more than conquerors through him who loved us. For I am sure that neither death nor life, nor angels nor rulers, nor things present [or past] nor things to come, nor powers, nor height nor depth nor anything else in all creation, will be able to separate us from the love of God in Christ Jesus our Lord."

I was overwhelmed to actually consider that there was a person around who would not leave me. A person who would stand by me, no matter what. Someone who could possibly end my separation anxiety. It sounded too good to be true. As I pondered this, there was an irresistible pull by the Holy Spirit telling me this all was true.

That was fifty years ago, and I can truly say, "*Yes*, it is true!" Nothing, no, nothing can separate us from the love of Jesus Christ. He has never left me. He has been with me through all of my life, the great times as well as the challenging ones, through all of it. Everything in my walk with Him has been a stepping stone on my way to glory. His love has been active and unchanging. I know He will always be there. What a change of experience for me—from death to life. All because of what He has done for me. Do you *know* without a doubt that He is always there for you?

Does your heart belong to Him?

Prayer

Dear Jesus,

Help me know and fully understand the depths of Your love and that You will never leave nor forsake me, no matter what. Instill in my heart and help me stand in the fact that nothing can separate me from Your love. Amen.

Reflection

____

____

____

____

____

____

____

Singing

I wonder, do you love music as much as I do? I find myself constantly singing. Sometimes when no one is looking, I not only sing, but I dance. In the car with the windows rolled down (at stoplights or just sitting in the car), at the gym, in my living room, when writing. I am quite sure people think I am nuts. Still, it doesn't stop me. Who cares?

Music has been a lifesaver for me throughout my life. I played piano for many years, playing classical and popular. There were times I wrote my own arrangements of popular songs. My piano teacher's desire for me was to carry on in music and apply to a very prestigious music school for piano and voice. I didn't. Life got in the way. Do I wish I had? Probably.

It had once been my outlet to get away, if only in my mind, from an abusive home life. After high school, I put music on the back shelf for a number of years. Just as music had once been a therapy for me, it seemed it no longer brought me the joy it once had. When I moved out of my family home in my late teens, I thought life would be easier. However, this was not the case. I had to do all I could to survive life.

It took until my early twenties for the Lord to get my attention. Up until that point, I wasn't listening to His Holy Spirit speaking to my heart, mind, and soul. It was a number of years after the Holy Spirit led me to faith and I gave my heart and life to my Savior, Jesus Christ, that a friend shared the verse Zephaniah 3:17 (ESV) with me. It states, "The Lord is in your midst, a mighty one who will save; he will rejoice over you with gladness; he will quiet you by his love; he will exult over you with loud singing." Now, not just singing, but *loud* singing. According to my Bible reference notes, this delight is grounded in the character of God, who "delights in steadfast love" (Micah 7:18, ESV).

I don't know about you, but I sure don't feel I give Him much to sing over me for, and certainly not loud singing, gladness, and rejoicing—a totally unbelievable concept to me. Yet, Scripture does not lie because my sins are covered by His death on the cross. Scripture says so, so I must believe it. Perhaps that is why music entered my life again. Now my singing and dancing have a purpose: joy and overwhelming gratefulness for what He has done for me and continues to do. Who wouldn't want to sing and dance over that?

Prayer

Dear Jesus,

I cannot fathom that You sing over me, but You do. Of this, I am assured because Scripture says so. Help me be thankful for knowing this truth. Let me sing with joy of your salvation and Your wondrous works.

Reflection

____

____

____

____

____

____

____

Speak

When I was growing up, I saw my dad as authoritative and having the final say about just about anything. When he spoke, there was no backtalk and generally no discussion. I had difficulty with this because I always wanted to challenge the information I was given. Now, this wasn't just when it came to my dad. As I grew up, this carried over into all areas of my life. My mouth had a hard time staying quiet.

When the Holy Spirit called me to a saving knowledge of Jesus, I thought it best to question anything and everything. I wanted to argue all the time. Perhaps it was because my friends told me that God was my Father, and for many years, I had a challenging relationship with my earthly dad. Then, some kind and thoughtful friends told me of some scriptures they thought I should read and digest. I was up for that, even though it may have required me to make some thoughtful changes.

They started out sharing Mark 4:35–41 (ESV). This portion of Scripture says that Jesus and His disciples left a crowd of people on the shore of the lake they were on. They decided to go across to the other side of the lake. While they were doing this, a great windstorm arose, and the boat began to fill with water. The disciples were in a panic, but Jesus slept. They woke Him and criticized Him for not caring about what was going on. Okay, here comes the rub. Jesus rebuked the wind and said to the sea, "Peace, be still," literally meaning, be muzzled. And there was a great calm. The next scripture my friends shared with me was Psalm 46:10 (ESV), "Be still, and know that I am God." In other words, keep quiet! Uh oh. I knew this was going to be a difficult task for me to do.

Over the years, I have come to realize that I can sometimes talk too much. And, when I am talking, I am not listening. Hebrews 2:1 (ESV) says, "Therefore we must pay much closer attention to what we have heard, lest we drift away from it." Pay close attention to His voice. Be still and know that He is God. Just be still!

I plan on continuing to work on this area of my life, probably until I see Jesus face to face. I see a long road up ahead for me in that area. That's all right, as long as I listen more than I talk and pay close attention to what I hear Him saying to me. I need to just be still and watch Him work in calming the storms in my life and calming me. I so thank Him for His patience, forgiveness, and grace.

Prayer

Dear Jesus,

Thank You that You know my heart of hearts so well. I am self-centered and lack humility from time to time. When You show me these times, help me to listen more than I talk. Teach me to be still and know that You are God.

Reflection

Standing Still

I am not much for standing still. When I was younger, my parents would have hissy fits because I could not or would not sit still. I am afraid that this characteristic has carried over into my adulthood. Frequently, friends (and others) will tell me to relax and *stand still*. Over the years, I have worked on this and still am, albeit I am much better now than ever before. I tend to be a busy bee. Why? I love life and want to experience as much of it as I can before I see Jesus face to face. I plan on living my life this way—from cradle to cross.

You may be wondering how this plays into this devotional. Allow me to explain.

There was a time in the Bible when the sun stood still. Did you know that? The story is found in Joshua 10:12–14 (ESV). Joshua needed help to defeat his enemy, so he petitioned God's help. Joshua 10:12 (ESV) says, "At that time Joshua spoke to the Lord in the day when the Lord gave the Amorites over to the sons of Israel, and he said in the sight of Israel." Joshua knew the power of God; he knew God could do anything, so he prayed. He knew God had a plan, and he wanted God to fight the battle. Joshua needed daylight to defeat his enemies during the battle, so he asked God to make the sun stand still. And, guess what? God did it. God was on his side and fought the battle for him. Joshua 10:13–14 (ESV) says, in part, "The sun stopped in the midst of heaven and did not hurry to set for about a whole day. There was no day like it before or since, when the Lord obeyed the voice of a man, for the Lord fought for Israel."

Is there a battle you are facing that seems insurmountable? Are you looking to Him to fight for you? Second Chronicles 20:15 (ESV) says, "Thus says the Lord to you, Do not be afraid and do not be dismayed at this great horde, for the battle is not yours but God's." Ecclesiastes 9:11 (ESV) says, in part, "Again, I saw that under the sun the race is not to the swift, nor the battle to the strong"…for Jesus Christ. Exodus 14:14 (ESV) says, "The Lord will fight for you, and you have only to be silent." Deuteronomy 1:30 (ESV) says, "The Lord your God who goes before you will Himself fight for you." And Nehemiah 4:20 (ESV) says, "Our God will fight for us." Are you catching my drift?

For way too many years, I tried to fight my own battles, not realizing God was always there waiting on me to pray and ask Him to fight for me. When we do this, we can rest and relax, knowing the battle is His. Are you willing to take note when you are fighting on your own? Are you willing to ask God to step in? Are you willing to stand still and wait on Him? I would highly recommend it!

Prayer

Dear Jesus,

Please forgive me for the times when I feel I am in the battle alone and for not asking You to fight for me. I know I will lose the battle without You. I know You are waiting for me to pray, ask and be silent. Holy Spirit, prick my heart when I am failing to ask for help in my battles.

Reflection

____

____

____

____

____

____

____

Step Out

Over the past several days, I have heard the phrase "out of my comfort zone" multiple times. It seems, to me, that this saying has become commonplace, enough so that, perhaps, it has lost its meaning. This morning I was at my favorite coffee shop with a friend and heard another catch-all phrase, "stepping out." Now, in my day, stepping out meant stepping out on someone, in other words, cheating. I laughed out loud to myself and joked with my friend when I said to her, "I am stepping out of my comfort zone!"

Peter knew all about stepping out. In Matthew 14 (ESV), Jesus instructed Peter and the other disciples to get into a boat and go across to the other side of the lake while He stayed on shore, dismissed the crowd, and withdrew up to the mountain to pray. That evening, high winds and waves soon beat against the boat and drove it a long way from the shore. Jesus wanted to be in the boat, so He simply walked toward it on the water. The disciples saw this and had a panic attack, thinking they were seeing a ghost. Talk about drama! Jesus spoke to them and told them not to be afraid.

Peter witnessed Jesus' water-walking, showed his doubt about what was happening, and challenged (this is really what he was doing) Jesus to command him to come to Him. Jesus simply said, "Come." Basically, step out of your comfort zone. Peter did. Well, sort of. Matthew 14:30 (ESV) says that when Peter saw the winds (perhaps felt the wind blowing him all over the place), he became afraid. Peter was distracted, became fearful, and took his eyes off Jesus. What happened? He began to sink.

What are you afraid of? Perhaps it is a dream that is now becoming realized, and now the reality has set in. Or, maybe you have been praying for a door to be open to you, and it is now—you are frightened to walk through it. Maybe it is being single for years and seeing no mate on the horizon, and you fear living alone for the rest of your life. Have you taken your eyes off Jesus? Is fear sinking in? It will if you allow it.

Challenge yourself, no matter what, to not take your eyes off Jesus. Watch Him walk on the water of your life, and don't lose hope. Don't lose sight of the fact that if Jesus could walk on water in the midst of the wind and waves, He will allow you to do that too. Trust Him. Don't give up. Step up and out of your comfort zone.

Prayer

Dear Jesus,

Please forgive me for those times I have not "stepped out" for You. I want to watch You walk on the water of my life and not lose sight of You and who You are. When I take my eyes off You, I begin to sink. I desire to trust You and not give up. Help me to keep my eyes focused on You.

Reflection

____

Take Me to the King

Recently, I underwent a four-hour medical procedure. I had this procedure done several other times, and each time, I was nervous and anxious. That morning, as in the past, I was feeling anxiety and some fear. I prayed and prayed; however, I did not feel much relief. I read my Bible before I left my home. The verses that were brought to my mind by the Holy Spirit were Matthew 11:28–30 (ESV). These verses state, "Come to me, all who labor and are heavy laden, and I will give you rest. Take my yoke upon you…and you will find rest for your souls. For my yoke is easy, and my burden is light." My burden that morning was heavy on my heart. I was feeling alone and miserable. I didn't know what to do. So, I simply asked, in my prayer, that my heart be taken to the king.

Who is this king? The king is Jesus Christ. The king is someone you can go to when you are weak and tired and when you feel you have no place else to go. He is there, and we are able to approach Him at all times. I was suffering and needed rest and comfort in my soul. My heart told me that morning that these verses were true and trustworthy, even if I didn't feel it. I was not alone.

That day, as I progressed through this test, I was able to focus my attention on Jesus. I prayed, I sang worship songs in my head (I didn't sing out loud because I didn't want to scare the nurses and techs), I talked to myself (again, in my head), telling myself the truths I knew about Jesus and who He is, I talked to everyone in my room about Jesus and who He was in my life—I did everything I could think of to keep my focus on Him. Guess what? It worked!

Are you going through a difficult time right now? Are you feeling alone, burdened, and heavy-laden? Look to Jesus, and you will find rest for your soul, for His yoke is easy, and His burden is light. Choose Him. He is always there, waiting to hear from you.

Prayer

Dear Jesus,

Thank You for the times when I feel lonely and alone; You are always there. I know I can come to You at any time with my burdens. Thank You that Your yoke is easy, Your burden is light, and I will find rest for my soul. I always want to choose You.

Reflection

____

____

____

____

____

____

____

Take a Look

This morning I heard a song that brought me back to a place where I was a long time ago. The song spoke of looking back at all the things I've done in the past that I am ashamed of—when I was a slave to my own desire and controlled by others. Romans 6:20–21(ESV) says, "When you were slaves to sin, you were free from the control of righteousness. What benefit did you reap at that time from the things you are now ashamed of? Those things result in death!" This passage goes on to say, "But now that you have been set free from sin and have become slaves to God, the benefit you reap leads to holiness, and the result is eternal life. For the wages of sin is death, but the gift of God is eternal life in Christ Jesus our Lord" (Romans 6:22–23, ESV).

Often times I consider what God has done in my life and how He brought me up from the miry clay into a saving knowledge of Himself, only because of His grace. The shame of the past is gone. He has made me new. Second Corinthians 5:17–19 (ESV) says, "Therefore, if anyone is in Christ, he is a new creation; the old has gone, the new has come." I have been reconciled to Him in Christ Jesus, and my sins are no longer counted against me. He has made me a new person. He uprooted the deep-seated lifestyle I was in and healed my wounds.

I think we all have a tendency, from time to time, to live in the past. For some of us, that might be fighting the urges to move back to past behaviors; for others, it may mean feeling negative and not being able to be positive about ourselves. Yet, for some, it might mean looking at how we were treated in the past (or now) and not being able to forgive. Not forgiving keeps us stuck in the same place in life, sometimes for years or until we die.

For me, I have struggled with all of these. During these times, I turn to Scripture to see what it says about me and God's grace. I also turn to trusted friends. Oft times, this means I must take a hard look at myself and stand firm in who I am in Jesus Christ. How about you? Do you need to take a look at yourself and your station in life right now? I encourage you to do so. What you do, and find, will be life-changing.

Prayer

Dear Jesus,

I thank You that You bring me to points in my life where I realize I am not where You want me to be. I praise You for these times because they draw me back to You and Your Word. Thank You, thank You, and thank You.

Reflection

Taking Steps

I love Winnie the Pooh, Tigger, and Eeyore. I have since I was very young. Winnie is the eternal optimist. Tigger just likes to bounce and have fun. For Eeyore, it seems he just can't get past the negative.

There are so many hardship stories in the Bible. Take Joseph, for instance. He was favored by his father, hated by his brothers. In fact, his brothers threw him into a pit and sold him into slavery. Then there is Job—a man of great wealth who had everything (and I mean everything) taken from him, his home, his livestock, his children, even his friends came against him. And how about Ruth, who took a chance and moved to a strange land with her mother-in-law after losing her husband. Esther took a chance and went before the king without being summoned. Then there was Daniel, who would not eat what the king told him to and refused to pray and bow down to anyone other than God. He was thrown into a den of lions. All of these people took a chance and did what they had to do to stay right with their Lord. These people lived through their circumstances and situations. Unlike Eeyore, we have nothing to complain about.

God is honored when we take a step of faith and trust Him. Joseph, Job, Ruth, Esther, and Daniel (and many others in the Bible) all took a chance in their negative situations, trusted God, and took a step of faith. The result? They were saved and honored. *And* their Lord God was exalted, honored, and glorified.

Ephesians 5:16 (ESV) tells us to be careful how we walk, to make the best of our time, and to make the most of every opportunity. Is there something you are being called to do and have been playing the role of Eeyore? If so, will you be willing to be a Tigger, bouncing around, excited about the opportunity of serving your Lord? How about being a Pooh, the eternal optimist and joyful about seeing God work in unknown circumstances? As for me, I have played all these roles. I want to be Tigger and Pooh, not Eeyore. How about you?

Prayer

Dear Jesus,

So many times in my life, I am an Eeyore, whining and complaining, not seeing the positive in my life. I don't want to be that way. Help me change this trait into a positive, always praising and thanking You no matter what.

Reflection

____

____

____

____

____

____

____

Taste Buds

I love food. My mouth salivates when thinking about a coffee latte, salmon, cinnamon toast, a great hamburger, *cheese*, chocolate peanut butter cheesecake, fried chicken. Shall I go on? Although I love all these things, I don't eat them often, as I am one of those people who looks at food and gains weight. So, for me, they are not the best foods to eat. First Corinthians 10:23 (ESV) says, "'Everything is permissible'—but not everything is beneficial. 'Everything is permissible'—but not everything is constructive." So, there ya go. Guess I won't be attending any food tasting conventions any time soon.

However, there is one thing I long for and do eat and never get tired of. Psalm 34:8 (ESV) says, "Oh, taste and see that the Lord is good!" *The Matthew Henry Commentary of the Whole Bible* on *BibleStudyTools.com* indicates this tasting and seeing His goodness involves discovery as well as enjoyment. For example, hearing about a delectable dish is far less alluring and personal than seeing a picture of the finished product. Running a bite over the taste buds then takes it to a whole new personal level. Yum! *Matthew Henry Commentary* also goes on to say, "There's a difference when we taste and see—when we're involved versus remaining a sideline spectator. To taste involves testing or sampling; to see involves understanding or perceiving. The phrase *taste and see*, then, means "try and experience."

Believers in Jesus experience the taste of God's grace and goodness when we recognize His provision, care, protection, and blessings. Just like delighting in food that we love, we can delight in the sacrifice He made with His death and provision of salvation. Humans associate taste with pleasure and satisfaction.

My desire is for you to taste and see. I want you to experience what I have so that you may come to know Him as I do and have a full heart and soul knowing that He sustains you with His goodness, mercy, unsustainable grace, joy, peace, and forgiveness.

Will you taste and see?

Prayer

Dear Jesus,

Physical food feeds my body. That's wonderful and necessary. But I want the food that feeds my soul. Draw me closer to You as I search those things that feed my soul. Amen.

Reflection

Temptation

Temptation is a funny thing in how it approaches you, not in a funny ha-ha way, but in how it sneaks up on you at the most inopportune times and sometimes through the back door. Often times it is upon us before we realize it. I know this happens to me. Perhaps it happens to you, too. It might come from a conversation I hear, a television program I am watching, lyrics from a song I am listening to (not a Christian song), or some other source.

There have been many times in my walk with Jesus Christ when I have struggled with temptation. In these times, I have turned to the Bible. I read stories of people like King David, who struggled with lust; Job, who struggled with his situation and his friends' attitudes; Gideon, who did not take God at His word and continued to put out a fleece before Him. David gave in, Gideon gave in, but Job did not. Job hung unto his faith and what he knew was true and good about God.

The other day I was talking with a woman, and we were discussing 1 Corinthians 10:13 (ESV) and how she and I had been struggling with areas of our lives over the past few years. She has had more than enough challenges. I mentioned to her that sometimes I have a difficult time with the concept of Jesus not giving us more than we can handle and beyond our ability. I guess I was sort of complaining. Her response to me was a kind reprimand. She told me that if that was my thought pattern, I was not believing Scripture when it says we will have temptation, but He will provide the way of escape so that we will be able to endure it.

What is that escape? Reading the Bible, prayer, gratitude, praise, seeking counsel from good friends—thank God for friends like mine, who are not afraid to call me out on my thoughts and behavior. The question is, will I choose to roll around in my struggle, or will I choose the way of escape and hold onto His promises? Temptation will always be around, and so will His promises. When we hang onto our faith and what He has promised, we will be able to endure it. I don't know about you, but life seems so much easier when I choose faith over temptation. I don't want to be a David or Gideon but a Job. I hope you do too.

Prayer

Dear Jesus,

Thank You that I know my struggles in life are not in vain. You use them to draw me to a closer walk with You. Help me live my life like Job and not like David or Gideon. Always help me to choose faith over temptation. I know life will be so much easier if I do. Amen.

Reflection

____

____

____

____

____

____

____

Training

I don't necessarily like to work out and sometimes enjoy it more when it's over. I have a personal trainer. I used to be able to fake pulling a muscle and whining. However, he now knows me too well and just laughs at me, much to my dismay. First Timothy 4:7–8 (ESV) says to train ourselves for godliness, for, while bodily training is of some value, godliness is of value in every way. It holds value for today but also for the life to come.

Sometimes I find myself faking and whining about how painful it sometimes can be to grow spiritually… Jesus, why do I have to go through this, why do I have to suffer, why should I read your Word every day, why should I pray when there are times it seems You don't answer, sometimes for years? Why bother? Doesn't He know anyway? I fall so short of doing what I should be doing in obedience and growing spiritually. Second Timothy 3:16 (ESV) states that all Scripture is breathed out of God and is profitable for teaching, reproofing, and training in spiritual growth. Why? Because Scripture, praying, and fellowship are all the ways I grow spiritually and become prepared for every good work He gives me to do. Just like my desire to become physically more fit, I should be even more desirous of continuing to become more spiritually fit. Where do you stand?

Prayer

> Dear Jesus,
>
> I long to exercise my spiritual muscles as well as my physical muscles. You know I fall short. Teach and show me when I am falling down on the job and help me get back on track.

Reflection

____

____

____

____

____

____

____

Trust

In this ever-changing world, it is difficult to put one's trust in anything. In my opinion, our society has become one of entitlement, selfishness, and "me first." How did we get to where we are? I have seen the changes come slowly, as our family structures have broken down, greed has taken over, and road rage is prevalent because my "stuff" is more important than yours. How sad—how it must grieve the heart of God.

For those of us who have a personal relationship with Jesus Christ, He has called us to something different. We are to exhibit the love of Christ, reach out to those who don't know Him, show grace and forgiveness, and most of all, put our total trust in the one who has shown reckless love in pursuing us.

Proverbs 3:5–6 (ESV) says, "Trust in the Lord with all your heart, and do not lean on your own understanding. In all your ways acknowledge Him, and He will make straight your paths." God's Word is the authority for all truth, not human beings. We can try until the cows come home to change this reality, but God is not in the market to change His plan.

Malachi 3:6 (ESV) says, "For I the Lord do not change." Even though the world around us is changing, we can rest and trust in the fact that He never does.

How wonderful!

Prayer

Dear Jesus,

Often times I find myself trusting in things that are not worthy of my trust. I want to only trust in You, for You do not change. Amen.

Reflection

____

____

____

____

____

____

____

Unchangeable Character

It has been a while since I have done any consistent writing. There are reasons for this; however, there should be no excuses. Please allow me to elaborate…

Several days before I was scheduled for knee surgery, I was told a lab test came back not so good. My surgery would have to be postponed for a month. Change in my life, again! I am finding I don't like so much change. So, as it should have been, I was to lay low during this period. I thought I would use my time wisely and do some writing. Well, guess what? That didn't happen. Instead, I spent the majority of this time being unproductive, discouraged, and sometimes fighting anger. The past close to three years have been challenging for me in a number of ways. I have, for the most part, been unable to exercise as I had been used to doing because of my knee problem. As I perused this past time, I went through a number of different stages of thinking. Did I create this situation?

Was I being punished by the Lord? Did He know what He was doing? You know, all the things we all ask ourselves when life doesn't give us what we planned or counted on. I'd like to say that I was faithful to doing my journaling and writing, having my quiet times, and praying, but I wasn't all the time. So, I decided this morning to do just that. I got out my Bible, prayed, and opened it. Here is what I found.

Hebrews 6:17–18 (ESV) states that His character and purpose are unchangeable; therefore, it is impossible for God to lie (what He says, He does, or will do), and that we need to hold fast to the hope set before us. Hmmm, unchangeable purpose and character and hope. What a wonderful promise for all of us. Even me. So, if His purpose cannot change, that means all the situations that have crossed my path these past several years are not in vain. Hallelujah! What a comfort! What hope and encouragement this brings to my soul.

Guess I am ready to meet life's challenges with strength, courage, purpose, and faith, knowing that nothing touches me other than those things that have passed through His nail-scarred hands. Hallelujah, again!

Prayer

Dear Jesus,

I am so thankful that Your character is unchangeable. I know I can count on this because the Bible says it is true. So, even when my life changes and I don't understand Your ways, I know I can rest in You and learn patience over and over again.

Reflection

____

____

____

____

____

____

____

Unexpected Surprise

I was recently encouraged to take a spiritual gifts assessment. Over the years, I have taken several, but it had been quite some time. So, I decided I would give it a shot. The results gave me my three top gifts. Much to my surprise, my top score was evangelism, different from the other assessments I had taken in the past. I scoffed a bit at this, though, because I usually think of those with the gift of evangelism as being missionaries or people who go door-to-door talking with people and handing out tracts. Or, perhaps, someone who drives around in their car with a loudspeaker blaring, "Jesus saves." Many of you are aware of these things or heard of them being done. I know I have. I don't usually think of simply sharing my faith as evangelism. You may think this, too. However, one experience changed my view.

I just had to get out of the house, so I decided to drive to a local coffee shop. I took my Kindle with me to do some reading and enjoy the weather. I decided to sit outside—no one was there, and the weather was simply gorgeous.

I had been reading for about an hour when a young lady who worked there came outside to clean a table. She came over to me and asked if I needed anything. She was young and very sweet. We started chatting, and I asked if she was a college student. "No," she said. She had just graduated from high school. She told me that she was hoping to go to a Bible school in England soon. Uh oh… That perked up my ears. I asked her if it was Capernwray, which is where I attended Bible school. She said, "*Yes!*" This "*yes*" led to a conversation about her former church, her former pastor and his wife, etc., etc. We knew the same people and some of our best friends were from the same families. We talked and talked. As we did, I occasionally looked around at several tables that were now occupied. I saw people watching us and listening to our conversation. I don't think she noticed, but I did. At the end of our conversation, I told her that I would be praying, that God would bless her with attending Capernwray. As she walked away, I again noticed that there were a few people still looking at us and talking among themselves. I can't say what they were talking about, but I believe some of their discussions dealt with what they had been eavesdropping on—Jesus.

I learned a lesson that day, or perhaps, relearned one I had forgotten about spiritual gifts. We never know what Jesus has planned for us each day. I surely didn't. I walked away feeling encouraged for having used my gift and sharing my faith and the joy of the Lord with a young eighteen-year-old. I anticipate what the Lord might do in the lives of those who were around us and pray for them. A double blessing! What is your gift? Are you using it? Check out 1 Corinthians 12 (ESV).

Prayer

Dear Jesus,

You tell us in Your Word to use our gifts and to not be afraid of doing so. I know I sometimes feel that I don't use mine to the fullest. Help me to take advantage of every opportunity You place before me. I want to honor You in all I do. Amen.

Reflection

____

____

____

____

____

____

____

Voice

What does "voice" mean in biblical terminology? The voice of God is His communication with us, heard as a sound with no apparent physical source. How does He do this? Through the Holy Spirit, who opens His way into our hearts. The Holy Spirit communicates to our hearts.

As I look back on my life before the Holy Spirit called me into a saving knowledge of Jesus Christ, I see the Spirit's working in my life for a long time. For years, I ignored His voice to enter the sheepfold. I had no knowledge of who Jesus was or what He had done, as I was forced to attend a church that taught nothing of the saving knowledge of Jesus. I quit attending church when I was in my mid-teens. As I see it now, God was showing me in the Bible who Jesus was, but I chose to push it aside. I remember coming across verses in the Bible talking about sheep, such as John 10:14–15 (ESV), John 10:3 (ESV), and John 10:2 (ESV). All of these verses say that He calls His sheep by name and that He knows them. Jesus calls Himself the Good Shepherd and that He cares for His sheep. To be honest, I could have cared less.

It wasn't until I was in my early twenties that I thought perhaps I should start investigating who Jesus was. So, I started reading the Bible, starting out with the Gospels, Matthew, Mark, Luke, and John. Through these books of the Bible, I began learning who Jesus was and what He had done for me. His voice, through the Holy Spirit, became loud and clear. He was calling me as one of His sheep.

John 10:27–28 (ESV) says, "My sheep hear my voice, and I know them, and they follow me. I give them eternal life, and they will never perish, and no one will snatch them out of my hand." I am in awe and humbled at the impact these verses still have on me after so many years. The statement "My sheep hear My voice" is packed full of wonderful news. If I listen, it tells me that Jesus wants to bring me into a personal relationship with Him. It states that Jesus died for me and that I can have a new life with Him. It says, without a doubt, that He has the gift of eternal life for me so that I may live eternally with Him.

Revelation 3:20 (ESV) tells us that Jesus stands at the door of your heart, waiting to be welcomed in, "Behold, I stand at the door and knock. If anyone hears My voice and opens the door, I will come in to him and eat with him and him with Me."

Although this verse in Revelation deals with the church, it can also be applied to us. Is the Holy Spirit calling you into a personal relationship with Jesus Christ? Is there knocking at your door, and you are ignoring it?

Are you listening to the voice calling you? If you are not, I challenge you to be open to listening to that voice, read His Word, talk with those you know who know Him personally, and find a church that preaches the Word of God and attend services. Don't let years go by before you do. Trust me; you will be glad you did!

Prayer

Dear Jesus,

I want to hear Your voice and follow You. I desire to know You personally and spend eternity with You. Thank You for the knowledge that when I have a life in fellowship with You, nothing and no one can snatch me out of Your hand.

Reflection

____

____

____

____

____

____

____

Water

Each year, at my yearly physical, my doctor frowns at me and tells me I need to drink more water. He says that water is vital to being healthy and is an essential component of life. I smile and tell him I will try to do better.

Water is not only an important issue for us but is an important topic in the Bible. It is first mentioned in Genesis 1:2 (ESV), on the very first day of creation. It goes on to be mentioned 722 times in Scripture. Water is not only fundamental to our physical fitness but also our spiritual well-being and for us to be vibrant, healthy Christians.

In the Old Testament, water is mentioned to do some of these things: heal from leprosy (2 Kings 5:1–14, ESV); in the story of the flood (Genesis 6:17, ESV), as having the power to purify and provide deliverance and to destroy evil and enemies. Moses, in Exodus 14:21 (ESV), stretched out his arms over the sea, and it parted, providing an escape to freedom for the Israelites from Egypt—it was all about water. In the New Testament, water is mentioned in the miracles at Bethesda in Jerusalem, John 5:1–9 (ESV), and in the baptism of Jesus Christ. Ephesians 4:4–6 (ESV) says there is one body and one Spirit, and if we know Him personally, we are called to one hope that belongs to our call—one Lord, one faith, one baptism, one God and Father of all.

The Bible says Jesus is the source of living water. He extends an invitation to those who thirst. His body shed water and blood from His wound on the cross John 10:34 (ESV). Jesus speaks of living water in John 7:37–39 (ESV), stating that anyone who is thirsty should come to Him and drink, and rivers of living water will flow from them. This is a symbol not only of water but of the Holy Spirit. In John 4:10 (ESV), Jesus speaks to the woman at the well and invites her to drink the living water He has to offer and gain the eternal life it brings.

Jesus talks of the difficult times in our lives as water by saying in Isaiah 43:1–2 (ESV), we need not fear when we pass through the waters, for He is with us; He has called us by name, and we are His.

Water is spoken of as our source of eternal life. It is symbolic of having spiritual cleansing if we accept God's offer of salvation. It purifies our soul and offers us the gift of the Holy Spirit. Water sanctifies us. It offers us freedom and sets us apart. Water not only purifies us and sets us free, but it also nourishes and gives us new life.

Water is crucial to our lives, both physically and spiritually. Without it, we will not survive here on earth or eternally. Do you drink enough water for your physical well-being? If you haven't already, are you willing to drink the water Jesus has to offer you for your spiritual welfare and to gain eternal life? If not, I pray you will consider this.

Jeremiah 17:13 (ESV) says Jesus is called the fountain of living water, and in Revelation 21:6 (ESV), Jesus claims that to the thirsty, He will give from the spring of living water of life—to those who believe and call Him Lord.

Prayer

Dear Jesus,

Thank You for Your gift of water and for nourishing our bodies and souls. Help me to be more aware of this gift and to be better at thanking and praising You for it. Amen.

Reflection

____

____

____

____

____

____

____

Wealth

For me, from time to time, finances are tight, as I am sure they are for you. This is a difficult and trying world we live in. I found about a year ago that I had to take on a job after not working for five years since my retirement because of this. Ugh. Because of limited finances, I had been unable to tithe as much as I had been. This was breaking my heart as giving is what I love to do. I have been disappointed in myself and have felt that the Lord is disappointed with me, also. Just at the right time, my pastor spoke on 2 Corinthians 9:6–15 (ESV), which says that each one must give as he has decided in his heart to give. Well, initially, this confirmed my guilty feelings. But, wait! He went on to say that these verses are not only related to money. They relate to time, serving, and praying. It is our attitude of heart, not money.

The Lord doesn't care about how much money I make… He cares about my heart and my understanding of the grace He has blessed me with. Instead of feeling guilty, I need to be thankful that He has given me a job, for however long I need it, to make ends meet.

So, where is the guilt coming from? Certainly not from the Lord! Jesus wants me to understand that my wealth does not come from money but in fully understanding that all my wealth is in the cross. Amen to that!

Prayer

> Dear Jesus,
>
> Knowing that You are more interested in my attitude of heart than the money I can give back to You helps me to see and understand where my wealth comes from. It is in the cross!

Reflection

____

____

____

____

____

____

____

What Was He Thinking?

I love considering myself a lifetime learner, and my heart wells up with overwhelming joy when I see others grow and learn. I have worked teaching adults in a prison setting and also taught college. However, one of my favorite groups is working with elementary school children. For many years I have tutored reading and writing to second through fifth-grade youngsters.

Right now, among several others, I tutor a young man in fifth grade. I began my work with him while he was in the second grade. When we started, he was in a charter school. He did not do so well there, so his parents moved him to a Christian school. Part of this young man's homework each week was to read a Bible story, answer questions, and then memorize scriptures. One day we were reading one of his Bible stories when he stopped mid-way through and asked me if he could ask me a question. "Why, of course," I replied. He went on to ask me if I knew that Satan was a fallen angel and that he fell because he wanted to be God. He stated that God sent him to his "own" place where he would live for all eternity. We talked a bit more, and then he adamantly made this statement about Satan wanting to be God: "What was he thinking?" with as much emphasis as he could muster. I tried my best not to laugh out loud. He had a great point.

Sometimes I get discouraged when things get tough, and I wonder just where God is. There have been times in my life when the negative things (or what I perceive as negative at the time) seem to far outweigh the positive. I feel like the devil is doing the two-step all over me. He (the devil) works hard to discourage and take us from our faith. God's Word says, "Little children, you are from God and have overcome them, for he who is in you is greater than he who is in the world" (1 John 4:4, ESV).

This speaks of discernment in dealing with things that are not of God and not letting these things get the better of us. I need to see quickly what the devil is doing and say to him, "Who do you think you are, and what are you thinking?" "For, greater is He who is in me than he who is in the world!" (1 John 4:4, ESV)

Prayer

Dear Jesus,

I pray that during the trying times when I find myself discouraged and Satan is doing the two-step all over me, I will look to You and say out loud, "Get thee behind me, Satan." You, and only You, are the author and finisher of my faith. Thank You! Amen.

Reflection

What's in a Name?

Think back to when you were younger, perhaps in elementary, junior, or high school, especially when it came to the opposite sex. Was there a schoolmate that you wanted to notice you? Talk to you? Ask you on a date? For me, it was usually hoping that he knew my name, if nothing else. For some of us, our world revolved around this. Our insecurities seemed to, at times, run our emotions. Having someone know our name was the ultimate goal.

As I became older, that desire did not change. I longed to be accepted for who I was, loved unconditionally, and appreciated. For me, that acceptance was not easily recognizable. I became a "yes" person, feeling that if I always said yes, acceptance would be just around the corner. Instead, what happened was just the opposite. I felt taken more advantage of, less loved, less accepted. Saying "no" to anyone was always at my own personal expense. Then something happened to change this.

In my very early twenties, I met a young woman who told me that she knew someone who would give me everything I needed, and did I want to meet him? Yes! She took me to a coffeehouse where a number of young people, like us, were meeting. They began talking about Jesus and how He knew them by name and how He loved them unconditionally. They shared that their past made no difference to Him. I became angry as I listened to them. I got up and walked out of the meeting. However, something kept driving me back to this place. It took about six weeks to get over my anger and hesitancy about this "whole thing." I began to realize that they were speaking truth. I decided to take "a chance on Jesus."

It is now over fifty years later, and I still walk with Jesus. I have learned, in real-time, it doesn't matter if others know my name; it only matters that He knows it. Isaiah 43:1(ESV) says, "But now thus says the Lord, he who created you, O Jacob, he who formed you, O Israel: Fear not, for I have redeemed you; I have called you by name, you are mine."

Does Jesus know your name? Do you know His? Do you want to know Him? It's not too late. Claim Isaiah 43:1 (ESV) as His promise to you, right here, right now. Allow the Holy Spirit to guide you into a saving knowledge of Jesus Christ. Come, share the gift of eternal life with me. You will never regret it.

Prayer

Dear Jesus,

I long for someone to know my name and know me intimately. I know. You know I do. I will share eternity with You. I want this for others. Help them know this truth in their heart of hearts and gain the gift of eternal life.

Reflection

____

____

____

____

____

____

____

When the Sand Runs Out

I am not a runner. In fact, I have never had the urge to run a race, be on a track team, run sprints, or anything else having to do with running. Maybe that is because I don't remember ever seeing a runner with a smile on their face. Hey, but that's just me.

However, Scripture tells me that I am not to avoid running. First Corinthians 9:24 (ESV) tells me that all runners compete, but only one receives the prize. Therefore, I am to run so that I obtain the prize.

Then there is Hebrews 12:1–2 (NIV), which says, "Therefore, since we are surrounded by such a great cloud of witnesses, let us throw off everything that hinders and the sin that so easily entangles us, and let us run with perseverance the race marked out for us. Let us fix our eyes on Jesus, the author and perfecter of our faith." What is this saying to me? I am to run the race set before me with fortitude, laying aside every weight and sin that clings closely to me, always looking to Jesus, who is the founder and absolute of my faith. Why am I running? To obtain the prize of knowing my Lord and Savior better and better each day and to have eternal life when the race ends for me.

My goal when the sand runs out is to know that I have run the race to the fullest. Just the thought of this happening pierces my heartstrings. Am I at this point in my relationship with Jesus Christ? Do I want, more than anything, to run the race until completion so that I obtain the prize? If not, what do I need to change to make this happen? Food for thought.

My thoughts and actions should be saying, "I have fought the good fight, I have finished the race, I have kept the faith" (2 Timothy 4:7, ESV). Am I ready for when sands run out? Will I be running the race as fast at the end as when I started? Will you be?

Prayer

Dear Jesus,

I long to finish the race strong. Help me put aside every hindrance, run without stopping, and receive the prize, eternal life with You. Amen.

Reflection

____

____

____

____

____

____

____

Without Wax

I often send my emails and letters to friends by signing "without wax." Years ago, I heard a pastor talk about the history of this phrase, "without wax." I had never heard of these words. However, I admit that what he had to share never left me. It was a lesson well learned with lasting effects on my heart, mind, and soul.

Here goes the history, as it was told to me… There was a time (and still may be) when merchants would sell their pottery for very high prices. Sometimes, when producing the product or selling it, items would get broken or cracked. The merchant, of course, wanting to make the most money he could, would try to fix the break or crack. He did this by melting wax and filling the cracks. This allowed the item to be fixed and, to the naked eye, could not be seen. Dishonesty was widespread. However, when the item was held up to the sunlight, the breaks and repairs could be seen.

I must say, I do this carefully and thoughtfully. After all, my Christian walk is on the line when I declare these words to others.

So, what do these two words mean to me? First Timothy 1:5 (ESV) says, “The aim of our charge is love, that issues from a pure heart and a good conscience and a sincere faith.” Ephesians 5:15a (ESV) says, “Look carefully then how you walk, not as unwise but as wise.” These verses show my heart that I must be wise, making sure nothing contaminates my behavior, my actions, how I treat others, and my heart. All these things (and more) must be sincere, pure, and genuine. *And* I must be realistic in how I view these areas of my life. And honest about where I am at.

“Without wax”—quite the two words. They can be or could be life-changing. For me, am I allowing “things” and outside forces to contaminate my thoughts and behavior toward others, toward my relationship with Jesus Christ? Am I being as sincere as I can be? Or am I trying to hide the flaws, cracks, and breaks in my life from others? You know, you may be able to fool others, but you cannot fool Him. So, what do you say? Are you willing to live your life without wax?

Prayer

Dear Jesus,

You know my true heart and motives. I want to be sincere in all I do. I know I can't fool You even when I think I can. Please help me, through the power of the Holy Spirit, to live my life without wax.

Reflection

____

____

____

____

____

____

____

About the Author

Susan Elizabeth Butcher is a teacher of adults, having worked in a prison setting for many years. She graduated with her BA in human resources management from Trinity International University in Miami, Florida, and received her master's degree in adult education from Alverno College in Milwaukee, Wisconsin. She is a life coach, having been certified through the American Association of Christian Counselors, and is also a certified grief counselor. She has been a spokesperson for a crisis pregnancy center and was a guest speaker for the center on a Christian radio station in Fort Lauderdale, Florida. She is a seasoned Bible teacher, speaker, and published freelance writer. Susan is single and resides in Brookfield, Wisconsin.

Endnote

1 Dr. Babu Philip, "Perfect Peace," Christian Moral Stories, Accessed April 13th, 2022, https://christian.moral-stories.com/2014/02/perfect-peace.html

CPSIA information can be obtained
at www.ICGtesting.com
Printed in the USA
JSHW050436260522
26347JS00002B/5